SPIRITUAL PRESCRIPTIONS FOR HEALING 10 DISEASES AND CHALLENGES

BY DR. TIEN-SHENG HSU

Cancer • Strokes • Heart Attack
Diabetes • Liver Disease • Accidents
Pneumonia • Kidney Disease
Depression • Hypertension

SPIRITUAL PRESCRIPTIONS FOR HEALING 10 DISEASES AND CHALLENGES

BY DR. TIEN-SHENG HSU

Cancer • Strokes • Heart Attack
Diabetes • Liver Disease • Accidents
Pneumonia • Kidney Disease
Depression • Hypertension

© 2018 by Dr. Tien-Sheng Hsu

Published by New Awareness Network Inc.
PO Box 192, Manhasset, New York 11030
www.sethcenter.com
www.sethinstitute.org

Opinions and statements on health and medical matters expressed in this book are those of the author and are not necessarily those of or endorsed by the publisher. Those opinions and statements should not be taken as a substitute for consultation with a duly licensed physician.

Excerpted from the lectures of Dr. Tien-Sheng Hsu
Compiled by Zi-Lin Mao
Translated by Meng-Fen Grace Lin, Felicia Chen and Haley Kang
Copyright Manager: JoJo Chen
Cover Design: Michael Goode
Editorial: Rick Stack

About the Translator
Meng-Fen Grace Lin, a professor at the University of Hawaii at Manoa, a Seth reader and learner. "My cancer brought me to the Seth teaching, which opened my eyes to a world of possibilities and creativity. Translating this book is an example of a possible me and its value fulfillment."

Printed Book ISBN: 978-1-7325883-1-8
EBook ISBN: 978-1-7325883-2-5

CONTENTS

Chapter 1
Cancer: To Open Blocked Life Energy

I open my heart and ask myself, "How can I live a beautiful life? What does it mean to live a meaningful life?" Whether or not you believe in reincarnation, you exist in this life as a unique being, within the vast universe. You are different than the you from past and future incarnations. There was no "me" before me, and there will not be a "me" after me. This is such a short and unique life that you must decide now how you will live it.

I once visited the historical home of the Father of our nation, Dr. Sun Yet-Sen*. As I was browsing through the exhibits, I saw an old photo of Dr. Sun lying in his bed just before his passing at age 59. I teared up, thinking about the beautiful life he had lived. All of his life, Dr. Sun persevered with passion toward his goals. Even though he only lived to 59 years of age, his zest for life should inspire us all. What could be more worthwhile than living for our passions and goals?

Note: Dr. Sun was a Chinese revolutionary, the first president, a founding father of the Republic of China, and a medical practitioner. Sun played an instrumental role in the overthrow of the Qing dynasty during the years leading up to the establishment of a modern Chinese society.

From this perspective then, I think every minute and every second of our lives are more precious than diamonds. The universe may be eternal, but our time on earth is as fleeting as a blink of the eye. Time does not wait for us.

Limited Time on Earth is Actually a Gift of Life

What a different concept! If something has an unlimited supply, then we may not appreciate its value. For example, citizens in Goxiong City have to buy drinking water due to the poor water quality in that region. As a result, drinking water in that area is precious due to its limited availability.

If we could see our time on earth in the same way, as limited, then we could appreciate our lives even more. Such thinking may inspire us to utilize our potential more fully. Even though we have a limited time on earth, we have unlimited life energy and latent abilities. This is an important fundamental concept that I share with my cancer patients.

People are diagnosed with all kinds of diseases, including cancer. Such a diagnosis seems to remind patients that they might not live to be 90 or 100 years old, as they had previously expected. They might die in a few years. So, is this a gift or a punishment?

In the last Seth book, "The Way Toward Health," Seth mentioned that a lot of cancer patients exhibit the strength of perseverance. Even though they don't know how to get out of a difficult situation, they persevere one day at a time. Once diagnosed with cancer, they begin thinking about life itself. They must find their own life spark or die.

Life can be paradoxical. I often tell my cancer patients that the disease is here to awaken their souls, to open their eyes, and to encourage their spirituality. Maybe they have muddled along without aims. Maybe everyday is mundane and uneventful. Maybe they throw a tantrum, have an argument with someone, scold their child, or get really angry. But when they are diagnosed with cancer and realize that their life may end soon, they gain a different perspective on life. They realize that their time on earth is finite, limited! In the moment that they realize that their life may end, they live again.

Because of this idea, I take a different approach to healing cancer. I help my patients to understand that cancer is only an illusion to make them see that their time on earth is finite. Cancer is not meant to make people live in fear, to force them to take all kinds of alternative medicines just to stay alive. It is a gift of life, allowing those who have it to start asking themselves, "How have I lived my life up to this point?"

I see life as an amazing book, in which each page represents a day. In your own life book, how many pages have you turned? How do you feel when reading your life book? I am sure many people have the experience of laughing or crying when reading a book. How do you feel when you are close to the end of a book with only a few pages left? Maybe you are moved. Perhaps, you are reluctant to part, or maybe you are full of appreciation and gratitude. For example, in the book, "One Thousand Spring Days," the author documented how she met her husband, fell in love, and lived their lives together. The husband died of cancer after 10 years of marriage. Even though they were together for only a short while, those times for the author were like "one thousand spring days," full of friendship, love, and affection. For the author, each phase of life has its own exuberant vitality.

Cancer is here to awaken a person's vitality. It forces us to confront this question, "If I don't have much time to live, then how do I truly want to live?" We learn about life when we understand that where there is birth, there is death. This is similar in concept to the idea that "only after things are lost are they truly valued."

Healing Starts from the Mind
It is actually rather simple to apply the holistic princi-

ples of body-mind-spirit to healing cancer. I often stress that, no matter which disease you might have, healing the body alone is not the answer. We should try to take as little medicine as possible throughout our lives. The less medicine we take, the healthier we are. We can see this idea in aging. If we take less medicine, it means our body is healthy, full of energy, and its self-healing ability is active. Without medicines, our immune system can function better, and all internal systems can respond accordingly.

I believe healing, whether it is for cancer or other diseases, should start with our minds. We all know that the mind is the master of our body. Our mind, thoughts, emotions, and everyday feelings guide the functions of the body. If we learn how to have joyful minds and how to live meaningful lives, then our bodies will become healthier and healthier.

<u>Consider the following example of a retired soldier living on pensions.</u> When he came to see me, he had had no prior medical diagnosis. His belly is as swollen up as if he were 8-months pregnant. Because he is retired, he stays at home everyday having nothing special to do. His wife cannot stand such an unproductive, unmotivated, goalless lifestyle, and friction occurs between the two of them.

Many men have similar issues after their retirement. Their spouses tell me that they do not care about the loss of income from retirement. What they cannot stand is to see their husbands sabotage themselves. The husband spends time at home watching television and sleeping. Or, he goes out with friends drinking and playing board games. Such an uninspired lifestyle can influence the household atmosphere, and it might even become a bad example for the children. The wife is disgusted seeing all of this and has no respect for the person her husband has become. Some wives even choose to leave home, getting a job in another city or pursuing their own dreams. These wives want a husband who has ambition, goals, and who is willing to pursue their dreams.

The retired soldier feels that he no longer has his wife's love and respect. He wonders, "Why is my wife not by my side? Why can't she respect me? Why does she want to pursue her own path?" Even his children are grown and are now living their own lives. All these add up to feelings that he is at the end of his rope and that he is powerless. On the one hand, he hates his wife who does not love him anymore; on the other hand, he hates himself for being so unproductive. But he loves his wife so deeply that he fears the part of himself who hates her. Nevertheless, his pride will not allow him to express his need for her affection.

As a result, this retired soldier made his last move. He started to lose weight. His belly swelled up. There are several possibilities medically: severe liver cirrhosis, pancreatic cancer, liver cancer, or even colon cancer. It is possible that his abdomen might be full of cancer cells.

I hold his hands and say, "I know you are in pain." He immediately begins to cry, relating the story of his broken marriage. He could not humble himself to face his wife. He feels that he doesn't deserve her return. He blames himself for being useless, with no real accomplishments. He feels that he doesn't deserve his wife's love and companionship.

From a deep holistic perspective of body, mind, and spirit, he has trapped himself with no way out. His blocked vitality, having no way to express itself, has no choice but to transform into cancer cells. He is in pain inside, not knowing how to live on. He loves his wife very much, but he doesn't know how to express his love.

All Diseases are Due to the Blockage of Life Energy
From this example, we can see that all diseases are caused by the blockage of life energy, including high blood pressure, diabetes, arthritis, and rheumatoid arthritis. Cancer is the most catastrophic of all the diseases! However, I can guarantee you that it is not as severe as you think.

In trying to heal cancer, I like to emphasize the

importance of understanding the true nature of this disease. We need to understand that cancer is not only a cell's pathological change, but it is also caused by the unbearable pain in your heart. You are facing life's difficulties, but you are seeing no solutions. Your vitality has no place to express itself but to appear as cancer in your body.

I often tell my cancer patients that if they can open their trapped, blocked vitality, allowing their spirit to grow, they can heal their cancer. The foundation of this concept is simple. What is a cancer cell? It is a cell that grows in an uncontrolled manner. It definitely is not as lethal as everyone thinks. We have so much fear about cancer, because we don't understand how cancer cells think.

So, from the holistic perspective of body-mind-spirit, how do cancer cells think? What do they want? Cancer cells appear because this person's life energy is trapped. That is, the person is suffering and finds no way out. As a result, the cancer cells, which already exist within the human body, grow, spread, and metastasize. It appears that cancer cells want to kill you. In actuality, all they want is to guide you to the path of spiritual growth. They are trying to get your attention! If you are learning, growing, and finding ways to express your energy, then your cancer "will heal itself!" If you begin to grow spiritually, then cancer cells have no reason to continue to grow, because you are expressing your vitality. Cancer will only overtake you if you don't learn these new life lessons, if you don't gain wisdom. Cancer cells will grow if you continue to allow your life to be stagnated, if you continue to feel trapped, and if you feel powerless within your situation.

I will give you another example. In the East, many cancer patients have relationship issues with their mothers-in-law. The daughter-in-law feels obligated to take care of the mother-in-law. At the same time, she might also need to be the primary caregiver for her children. Often the daughter-in-law feels mental and physical exhaustion, and she desperately wants to let go of some of her responsibilities. However, she might have two conflicting voices inside. One voice might say, "It goes without saying that my mother-in-law is my responsibility." Yet another voice might remind her that she alone shouldn't have to be responsible for her mother-in-law when there are other daughters-in-law and sisters-in-law who are also available. Resentment and conflicting feelings bother her constantly.

In some cases, when the mothers-in-law are very sick, the daughter-in-law might have a little "hope." Maybe she can see a little light at the end of the tunnel. Often, however, the mother-in-law lives on, getting healthier by the year due to the great care of the daughter-in-law. The healthier the mother-in-law becomes, the more hopeless the daughter-in-law feels. She might fall into desperation, thinking, "How much longer can I live like this?" She might lose sight of her future.

Let's put the discussion of right and wrong aside. As a situation, how can this daughter-in-law find meaning in her life?

From my clinical experience, I have seen a lot of breast cancer patients who are stuck in this kind of relationship. They do a great job of being the caregiver of their mothers-in-law, but they are suffering tremendously. They have no way to release their pain; they feel trapped with no way out. If they cannot accept the situation and yet they have no ability to resolve it either, then their blocked vitality starts to seek alternative avenues.

Many people are fairly well-off but remain unhappy. Most of the time what is lacking is spiritual growth. This is a form of joy, and it is one's passion for life. When are we the most joyful? It is when we are learning, creating, and seeking new possibilities. It is when we can express our joy, our vitality, and our zest for life.

However, if a person is trapped in a difficult situation with no way out, the person's cells might mutate into cancer cells. I hope everyone fundamentally understands cancer. I never agree that cancer is caused by a person's physical makeup or by the food they have eaten. There is only one real cause of cancer: twisted spiritual vitality.

Cancer patients need to understand thoroughly that cancer is caused by their own twisted vitality. They then can start finding new life energy. When you are faced with death, you should ask yourself, "Do I want to continue living like this? If I have only three months to live, how will I choose to live it? Do I want to live earnestly? Happily? As a free spirit? Joyfully?" We must realize that much of our suffering and our constraints are self-imposed. We do this to ourselves.

Many cancer patients hold on to grudges, but they don't like to be a person who is full of hatred. It frightens them to think that they cannot control their hate. They are afraid that they might be capable of destroying people close to them.

I once had a liver cancer patient who confessed to me that he had given himself cancer in order to destroy himself. He was afraid that if he didn't destroy himself first, he might kill his wife. He realized that his hatred towards her had grown out of control. Due to his hatred and his feeling of psychological imbalance, he had completely lost himself in money, fame, and pleasures. He didn't know where he was headed. After talking to me, he realized that while he could destroy himself with his cancer, he could also save his marriage and his life. He could absolutely start anew. He decided to face his life; he chose not to continue to hold on to his suffering. He began to cry in my office, releasing all the pent-up feelings that he had accumulated for years.

Healing Cancer with the Mind
Only when we are trapped in such predicaments, will cancer occur. Let me emphasize this again. Cancer cells are trying to tell this person, "Timeout! Take a moment to consider how you want to live. Think about what is life."

I have some suggestions when treating cancer patients:

1. Begin Learning the Holistic Principles of Health
Cancer patients must begin to trust their own bodies. They must believe that their bodies are kind and friendly, and they must have faith that their bodies possess magical self-healing powers.

Nowadays, many people have poor health, and the important factor is because they have lost faith in the body's intelligence. I want to advocate for a "religion for all." This new religion would have tenets that include the following ideas: Our bodies possess the oldest wisdom in the universe; our bodies contain splendid magic; our bodies have the most magnificent self-healing powers!

Next, everything you do is for the purpose of arousing the body's original mighty self-healing powers. Once the self-healing power is activated, once you have learned to trust your body, and once you understand that diseases are caused by the suffering in your mind and not through any fault of your body, then your faith in the body will increase exponentially.

You will not fear a weakening body, but, instead, you will experience the grace of living in a healthy body. I have great faith that we are born to be healthy, and we can recover from any disease. Once you have established this faith for yourself, I guarantee that your body will start activating what it needs to heal itself.

Maybe you will have a sudden craving for a certain food or an urge for a certain type of exercise. Your body suddenly gains its own rhythm and consciousness. Because of your trust and encouragement, your body will start to activate its own ability, and such an activation might even reach into the deep inner wisdom within each cell or its electromagnetic field.

Even your dreams might change when your body is in the self-healing process. In your dreams, your hormones might start to change, and your body might readjust its immune system. All the holistic concepts you have learned about body, mind, and spirit can be integrated during this process.

2. To Transform Your State of Mind

I have spoken of the following key concept: If your life and spirit begin to grow, your cancer cells will cease to grow.

There is no other way that is faster and can solve the root of the problem. Does radiation therapy work? It does. Radiation will shrink the cancer cells, but it will also kill the normal cells. Does chemotherapy work? Yes, chemicals are injected through your veins. The cancer cells will disappear, but so will the normal cells. In addition, you will lose your hair.

All these therapies can have an effect, but none gets to the root of the problem. If your life remains unchanged, if your mind continues to suffer, if your worldview remains the same, then your blocked energy will continue to seek other outlets for expression. This energy will continuously turn into cancer cells, and then you have to use radiation, chemotherapy, and drugs continually to constrain this energy. This is a lose-lose situation! Modern medicine is on this useless path.

There are even more drastic treatments available. For example, there is a therapy that exposes your entire body to an extremely high dose of radiation. This thera-py kills all of the cancer cells as well as all of your stem cells. Once all of your stem cells are killed, you must stay in a sterile room waiting for a bone-marrow transplant. This is an incredible gamble: You must be willing to die on the outside chance that you might live.

The truth is, the odds of survival are identical be-tween cancerous and normal cells. All cells breathe as you breathe. I often joke that it is simple to kill cancer cells. As long as you stop breathing for ten minutes, all of your cancer cells will die. Isn't this simple enough? But the point is that you will not live, either; cancer cells live and die with you. No medical treatment can kill cancer cells but keep you healthy. You and your cells are one. You drink a cup of cappuccino, so do your cancer cells. You then eat an all-you-can-eat lunch buffet and are satisfied. So are your cancer cells.

Similarly, if cancer patients take tonic supple-ments, these nutrients will go to the cancer cells as well as the normal cells. The more nutrients you take, the more energetic you may feel, but it will be the same with your cancer cells. So you see, we cannot kill only the cancer cells, nor can we provide nutrients to our normal cells alone. The only way to heal cancer is love. Use love as the treatment for cancer, and start by loving yourself.

3. Expand life experience

For example, start learning new things. Learn a new language such as Greek or Japanese, and then plan a study tour to Greece or Japan. Through experimenting with new stimuli, we can begin to live differently and even get to know ourselves differently.

I have a liver cancer patient whose dream is to become a scholar. Unfortunately, his family was devastated by the financial crisis, and he was forced to go into business. As a merchant, he insisted on obeying rules and being honest. He has worked hard all his life, but he has not earned much. Knowing that he has an apartment in Shanghai, I suggested that he let go of the business in Taiwan, fix up the apartment in Shanghai, move there, and enroll in the university as a student again. If he could do this, getting back to the university campus, immersing himself in piles of books, wandering back to the era of Romeo, who knows? He might just run into his Juliet. Anything is possible! If he could follow his dream and enter into a new environment, then he might have a brand new start in his life! If he were fortunate enough to find a new life, then his cancer cells would have no future. However, if he is still trapped in his mental suffering, then he gives his cancer cells endless hope.

Unfortunately, this patient did not succeed in the

end. He equated his work to his life, so he could not let go of his business. As a result, he did not embark on a new adventure, new possibilities, nor did his worldview alter.

4. Adjust Your Attitude toward Life

Regardless of what disease you have, adjusting your attitude toward life is a priority in the healing process.

Foremost, you must change your thought habits. You must learn to be more optimistic, seeing things from a more positive perspective. You must learn to enjoy the beauty of life.

Secondly, you must learn to observe your own emotions. You have accumulated too many conflicting, tangled, and painful emotions that are mixed with love and hate. You are emotionally confused.

If your doctor tells you that your cancer cells are malignant, what does this mean? Normal cells are very pretty, but cancer cells are twisted and spiral-shaped like knots in a rope. This is because your emotions have been twisted and out of control for a long time. This is mimicked in the cancer cells.

Reexamine and reflect on your emotions. Find an outlet for your contradictions, conflicts, struggles, and pains. If you calm yourself down, your cells will change accordingly. Through this process, your cells will look differently each time a biopsy is performed.

We have not yet realized our true potential. You must believe, "When I change my belief system, even my cells will change accordingly." True genetic engineering is not done in the lab but through the change of our beliefs.

Do you know the power of your mind? A single thought can change the entire universe! Through the change of a single thought, you can transform your hell-like suffering into a state of bliss. When you change your thought patterns, not only can cancer cells be changed, but you can also reverse any disease, including high blood pressure and diabetes.

For years I have studied the spiritual potential of humans, and I have reached a conclusion. If we can truly understand the power of our thoughts, if we can begin to see the holistic relationships among body, mind, and spirit, and if we are willing to begin to change, we will be able to experience the inconceivable power within ourselves. Perhaps, your thought patterns are getting outdated, and your emotions have stagnated. You feel that tomorrow will be a continuation of today's helplessness, boredom, and pain. It is an unappetizing life, but it is not yet bad enough to be thrown away. This is not life! Let every day be a new page in your personal Book of Life! Let every day be a new adventure! <u>You have no time to waste!</u>

For those who live day by day without purpose, let's start the change now! What more can you lose now that you have cancer? Let everyday be a new beginning!

Your Declaration to Your Cancer Cells

A cancer diagnosis leads us to an interesting thought, "What else is there to think about? I am going to die." Don't think too much <u>when initiating new actions.</u> This does not mean you can do whatever you feel like doing. Based on the principles of "Do no harm" and within the premises of the law, you are free to take any actions. You are ready to reactivate your own vitality.

Once you have reactivated your vitality, you are to declare to your cancer cells, "Hey, you! Do not be so cocky! Stop growing. I am the one who needs to grow. I am expanding my life circle. <u>I am redirecting my spiritual energy into productive paths. You stop!"</u>

Once you have awakened your passion and energy, then you have access to an endless supply of vitality. I equate treating cancer to encouraging spiritual growth, believing that spiritual vitality can have the power to heal diseases, such as cancer. I am trying to eradicate the misconceptions of treating only certain parts of our cancerous bodies by seeking famous doctors or by taking alternative medicines.

Our bodies do not need to be cured. All of the

treatments that focus exclusively on treating the body do not get to the root of the problem. You might see some improvement here and there with those methods. If that is the case, it is only because you spend time taking care of yourself, and you start to love yourself. You fear death, so you begin to be kind to yourself. You start to appreciate life. Those are the reasons why your body might begin to heal. It is not because of the various treatments or the specific supplements that you have taken.

Everything that you do to take care of yourself means that you want to live. This very thought can activate our body's self-healing ability. Please remember that our bodies do not need to be cured. They need your love and trust. Once your body has that, it goes into the self-healing process immediately.

The Transplant of Thoughts

How do we activate our vitality in the process of treating cancer?

Many people are trapped in their own egos and are inflexible with their existing thought patterns. I offer a new concept called the "transplant of thoughts." You let go of all your old belief systems and then "transplant new beliefs," which we will call a new thought system. With the new thought system in place, you begin to appreciate life, to see many possibilities, and even to see your own difficulties in a new light. You have a totally new perspective. You believe everything will have a positive ending. If we can begin the transplant of new thoughts, these new thoughts will activate new abilities within our bodies. Our body's abilities will then be activated through our new thoughts and beliefs.

You must remember this essential concept: Our vitality will not decrease as we age. This means that whether we are age 30 or age 80, we have the identical vitality. Most of us continue to learn until we are 30 years old, but then we slow down after that. Once we reach 50 years old, we probably live a life with the same old routine day after day. What happened to learning, adventure, challenge and creativity? They are gone! So where is our vitality used? It is used to create cancer cells.

Let's see how much energy cancer possesses. No one in the entire medical field knows what to do with cancer. Cancer grows back shortly after radiation. Chemotherapy almost kills the patient, but the cancer cells still grow back quickly. Some patients cut off both breasts, only to have the cancer spread to their ovaries. Even after an ovary is removed, the patient finds out she has lymphoma. If all the lymph nodes are removed, will the cancer spread to her lungs? It is no longer uncommon to have two cancers in one person at the same time.

I had a patient who came to see me for the first time three years ago. She was diagnosed with ovarian cancer and went through all of the standard medical treatments. However, she did not take the opportunity to have a complete makeover of her life. Six months ago, she came to see me again. This time, she had lymphoma. I have yet another patient who lost a breast four years ago due to breast cancer. She came to me a year ago with ovarian cancer.

When I was still a student in medical school, it was rare to have more than one cancer in the same patient. It is rather common now. Why? Mainstream medicine has not yet found the solution that can get to the root of the problem.

Cancer cannot be healed if we focus solely on treating our bodies. We must take the three-pronged approach, healing together the body, mind, and spirit. Cancer can be a disease of the past if all cancer patients could find their life's passion and joy.

Welcome to the Pantheon of Spirituality
We should all be awakened to the path of holistic spiritual growth. In today's society, many are pessimistic and have lost the meaning of life. Eighty percent of adults are not happy and cannot feel joy and ease in their lives. When entering into menopause and beyond, many women are fearful. More and more people

only want to live into their 60s. There is no point in living beyond that. For them, old age equals being useless, weak, and sickly. It means becoming a dependent and, therefore, a burden to others.

There is much fear around becoming old. However, these fears stem from the lack of spiritual growth and the adherence to old thinking patterns. If the way we think does not grow and expand, our life vitality cannot be activated. It then cannot be transformed into joy and interesting challenges. We will never learn to be a free spirit. Our endless supply of vitality will either energize us or kill us.

Cancer is here to force us to make that decision as to whether you want to live or to die. All the healthy regimens and advanced modern medicine will not cure cancer, not as long as we are unhappy, finding no joyful growth, lacking self reflection, and are deficient in the feeling of ease and enlightenment.

Through healing cancer, I wish to point people to the lifelong journey of spiritual growth, to understand the nature of our existence, to continue to absorb new knowledge, and to activate inner vitality. When we focus on spiritual growth, something magical will happen. Cancer will heal itself without any treatment! It should! As long as we understand this key concept of self-healing, diseases will heal without outside interference. I often claim that the body is its own best doctor. There is profound wisdom within our bodies.

Over the years, through my books and talks, I have been advocating this three-pronged approach to health which integrates body, mind, and spirit. I only wish to bring awareness to the importance of seeking spiritual growth. The journey into spirituality will help cure diseases if you are sick or make you healthier if you are already healthy. Your life will be completely changed.

Conversation with the Inner Self

I am very moved by this story. A student's father died of high blood pressure and a heart attack; cancer took her mother's life. When she visits them at the cemetery, she reads them my book "Connection Between Mind and Diseases," in the hope that her parents can learn and grow with her. She used to have migraines, but now the pain has subsided greatly. This is because she has begun the journey into her inner self. It might appear that she was talking to her parents, but she was actually having a conversation with her inner self.

I read a story in a medical journal about a man who had been allergic to strawberries since childhood. If exposed to strawberries, he could go into shock and die due to his allergic reaction. As a result, he pays very close attention to his diet. One year he visited Italy and went to a high-end restaurant for a meal. He made a special request to the chef to keep strawberries out of his food. The meal was served, the man finished eating, and nothing happened. Three hours later, he received a call from the restaurant. They said, "We are terribly sorry. Due to our negligence, there were strawberries in your food." Upon hearing this, he immediately went into shock and died.

Was he killed by his allergy to strawberries? No! He was conditioned to believe that it would be so. According to research, when a person is in a deep hypnosis and you tell him, "I am burning your hand with a lighter," his hand will have blisters on it after ten minutes. Do you see how strong our minds can be?

As soon as a child catches a cold and is uncomfortable, many parents rush the kid to see a doctor. In reality, many children just have nasal allergies or inflammation or have a skin rash. Unless it is absolutely necessary, I strongly suggest not using drugs such as steroids. Let me teach you a different method called "the magic pill."

Let's invite children to play an imagination game in which we will create a magic pill together. This pill will have miraculous power. When you swallow one, all of your health problems, whether it's a cold, a fever, asthma, or allergies, will be gone! Then have the children pretend that they have swallowed this magic pill.

Believe me, this magic pill is the most effective of all the pills you have ever taken. Our vitality and self-hypnosis can bring us back from death's door. I have taught this method to many people, who no longer need medicine to reduce a fever or to rush to the emergency room in the middle of the night.

Unlike the grownups, many children are still young enough not to be influenced by conventional thinking. Many children are still in touch with their subconsciousness. This magic pill's hypnosis instruction can easily reach deeply into their subconsciousness, or even unconsciousness, and quickly have a positive effect.

We focus too much on the material world and neglect the fact that our mind is the true master. Medicine will not bring you true health. If you truly believe in our magic pill, then start experimenting with yourself first. If you are a little sick, try not to take any medicine. Instead, take the magic pill. Then try this on your children and your grandchildren. This is a great game for all ages with astonishing results.

How to Grow Spiritually
There is only one key concept: Follow your impulses!

We all possess a buddha or a godlike nature. In the pursuit of spiritual growth, all we need to do is to follow our inner intuitions and the spontaneous joy of our own being. As we are more educated, we develop a more rational mind, and we repress more of our inner spontaneity and affection.

I have a cancer patient who is good at painting. She wanted to change her career, so I asked her, "How about integrating your artistic talents with the spiritual path that you are learning?"

She replied, "I don't know how."

I said, "It is very simple! If you really want to, the path will show itself."

Please remember that if you want to take the steps, the path will show itself. The external world is created through our inner beliefs. You must have the desire to walk down that path before the path will show itself to you.

Even though she was not clear about what I meant, she decided to have faith in herself. She gradually detached herself from her work. As it happened, we were having an exhibit of the artwork of our cancer patients. She started to reorganize her paintings, and she began to teach people simple sketching at the exhibition.

It is possible that this lady's life mission is to help sick people regain their vitality through the creation of art. She can teach sketching next to a patient's hospital bed. In that process, she also finds the meaning of her own life.

Why do we feel lonely? Why are we lost in life? It is because we cannot hear our inner voice anymore. A key to spiritual growth is to reconnect with our inner selves.

Seth mentioned that before we were born, we created our life's blueprint. Everyone has an inner GPS system that contains memories from all of their incarnations, including everything we have learned even before our current earth experiences.

Earth is not our first classroom for learning. Our consciousness existed before earth did. Our life blueprint, the inner GPS system, stores all the predispositions of our personalities.

Most parents would testify that each of their children is unique. Each has his own personality. Maybe one is outgoing, and another is shy. The path of spirituality is to uncover our life blueprint. The more we can live a life that is close to our blueprint, the more we can be at ease, be joyful, and trust our intuitions. We must not allow interference by outside noise.

Listen to Your Inner Voice

When you can listen to your inner voice and have faith in yourself, your inner vitality will carry you forward. All you need is to listen; do not resist your impulses. Simply follow the flow of your own energy. When you tap into your own inner vitality, you can then relax your ego, who thinks it has been all alone in making life decisions.

Seth is guiding us to our own inner vitality, to finding who we are. This is a path to enlightenment, self-reflection, growth, and the discovery of the miraculous powers that are our own. As we begin the journey into our inner world, our inner GPS system will guide us. You naturally know where life will lead you. You have faith in the universe, and the universe will provide guidance to you.

However, you still have to put in the effort to make anything happen. The difference is that you will feel steadier along the way. The more you can listen to your inner wisdom, the happier you can become. The earlier you start this journey, the more fulfilled you can be.

I often imagine immersing myself in the river of my inner vitality, allowing the joyful energy to guide me. I trust the kindness of the universe without any fear. I wish to bring this feeling of peace, ease, and joy to everyone. Let go of all worries, suffering, conflicts, and struggles. On a consistent basis, we all need to affirm our own goodness, to accept who we are, and to find more trust and love within ourselves.

When your life is full of joy, your mind will be calm, and you will have heightened awareness. If you can have faith in your body's self-healing abilities, you will also be able to trust your own ability and vitality. You will have faith that your life will be the best that it can be.

 with Dr. Hsu

Question: My daughter has recently been diagnosed with lymphoma. I was told by many that it is because I have not been paying attention to my daughter's diet. I blame myself and don't know what to do.

Response: Rest assured that diet is definitely not the cause of her lymphoma.

The real cause might be related to the stress that your daughter has endured. Maybe the stress comes from her schoolwork or maybe from herself. She is stressed to the point that she has much fear and anxiety; her sense of security has come to a complete breakdown.

Our lymphatic system is our body's security system. Its main function is to transport infection-fighting cells throughout our bodies. However, a person's feeling of extreme insecurity will shake its own body's security system. The cells backlash! The prescription for this condition is simple.

First, release the stress! Whether you have good

grades at school or not, accept completely your current ability.

Second, apply the teachings of spiritual growth. Start seeking your joy in life, instead of focusing on "getting things done."

How stressful would it be if you had to be "perfect" or had to achieve a certain standard to be considered successful? When the stress is too much, if you don't break down, your immune system will. When your immune system breaks down, then comes lymphoma.

Question: I was diagnosed with a malignant tumor in my lung. It has now spread to my left breast and my lymph nodes. The doctor suggested chemotherapy. I am not afraid of death, but I am afraid of pain. I worry that my cancer will spread again. I have taken Iressa, and I am currently taking detox supplements. Things seemed to be working at first, but after a few months, the cancer marker rose. Now that I have learned about the connection between body, mind, and spirit, I really don't want to undergo chemotherapy. Is this the right decision?

Response: I am neither for nor against your taking Iressa or detox supplements, because they are not the key. If you do take them, you might see a positive short-term effect. However, if you are not changed inside, it will make no difference what you take. From the holistic perspective, they are not a cure but temporary relief. The true cure starts with our minds.

First, let go of your fear of cancer, both the fear of death and the fear of pain. Let it go first. Then, ask yourself, "Do you have any regrets in life?"

From my clinical experience, older people who got lung cancer usually had regrets in their lives. They ask, "Do people around me love me for myself or for my accomplishments?" Maybe they are the most outstanding among all of their siblings. Maybe they are contributing the most to family affairs. In spite of these factors, they are not feeling loved. These older people have a lot of sorrow and pain that they are forced to suffer in silence.

Foremost, you must see your desire for love. You must process this emotion. Open your heart and feel that you have been accepted for who you are. Do they love me or my accomplishments? You must also process this emotion in a way that you will not be sorrowful. If you die, you want to die in peace and not with regrets.

Next, get on the path to spiritual growth. If you can find your passion and conscientiously face your fears, then cancer is nothing! The most important thing is to find the path to joy.

Be a child again. You can learn many things and do anything. Instead of longing for love, how about spreading love proactively?

Many possibilities await. Do not spend your time worrying about which treatment to take or which diet might work for you. Life should not be wasted on these things. Rather, find your joy in life.

Even if you die three months from now, you will feel that these last three months are the happiest ones of your life. Then life would be worth living. Whether it is tangled emotions or blocked vitality, you must find an outlet to express them. Love is of the highest importance. Allow yourself to love and be loved.

➤ Reminder from Dr. Hsu

Suppose you believe in reincarnation, and you also believe that each incarnation has its own goals, learning, and challenges. Suppose you die today, ending your soul's physical earth trip. Can you let it go? Are you satisfied with how you have lived? If your answer is that you still have regrets, then please do your best to live to your highest potential!

Chapter 2
Strokes: The Manifestation of the Feeling of Helplessness in Life

"The Wedding Banquet" is director Ang Lee's early work, exploring the issue of homosexuality and its impact on traditional family values from the Chinese perspective. The story starts when Chinese parents visit their son who is working and living overseas, in the hope that he will marry soon. What they do not expect is that their son is not only gay but also has an intimate boyfriend who lives with him. Bound by Chinese traditional filial piety, ethics and morals, the son does not reveal this truth to his parents. Because he is forced by his parents to get married, he chooses a Chinese girl who wants to get her green card through marriage.

The truth always comes to light sooner or later. The father finally discovers that his son is a homosexual through observing his interactions with his boyfriend and his new wife. Soon after the discovery, the father has a stroke! Under the great care of the boyfriend, who is a physical therapist, the father gets better day by day. In that process, he gradually accepts his "son-in-law."

Let's use this story as an example to discuss the reason for having a stroke. In the film, after discovering that his son is gay, the father does not expose this fact right away. Instead, he pretends that he does not know about it. However, this is a very heavy blow for him, as homosexuality contradicts his traditional values. It is beyond the father's imagination that his son loves another man. Is this the son I have raised with much hard work and of whom I am so proud? Because of this shock, the father's blood vessels burst, and he has a stroke! The stroke, however, is caused by the father's silence, even after discovering his son's true sexual identity.

In the film, the father, with very traditional Chinese values, comes to the realization that the next generation needs to walk their own path. With wisdom, the father accepts his son's sexuality and also accepts the "son-in-law" who has been taking great care of him. Because of this change, he is recovering from the stroke.

Why is the father recovering from his stroke in the film? From the holistic view integrating body, mind, and spirit, the biggest reason for the father's recovery lies in his willingness to change his point of view, to accept his son, as well as to accept the man whom his son loves. If the same thing were to happen to a different father, then the result might be different. For many people, their values are unshakable and inflexible.

We must change with the times and allow ourselves to be adaptable, to be childlike, to be interested in many things. We must live and learn. We must not be constrained by a rigid value system. From the holistic perspective, if a person has only one value system for his entire life, if he cannot accept others' suggestions, and if he is unwilling to understand others' points of view, then this person's cardiovascular system will begin to deteriorate. Therefore, a stroke is a holistic issue related to our mind, body, and spirit.

Strokes from the Medical Perspective
Strokes are a form of cardiovascular disease. High blood pressure, high cholesterol, high blood glucose, obesity, the lack of exercise, and so on are all related to cardiovascular disease. Strokes are among the most common health problems and contribute greatly to catastrophic illness and death among older people.

1. Transient Ischemic Attack (TIA).
The patient will recover within 24 hours. Symptoms include a sudden decreased level of consciousness, visual impairment, and unsteady gait. However, after recovery there are no residual effects, because the condition is caused by a temporary lack of blood supply in an isolated part of the brain due to a small blood clot. Because the clot is small, it only causes a temporary obstruction and will be dissolved quickly.

2. Stroke due to low blood pressure.
Most people think that it is only high blood pressure that causes a stroke, but they ignore the fact that low blood pressure may also cause one. If the blood pressure is too high, our blood vessels may burst. On the other hand, if the blood pressure is too low, we could also have a stroke due to insufficient blood flow to the brain. The brain cells die due to a lack of blood supply. That's why I always tell elderly friends, "Be careful not lo let your blood pressure drop too low." When the blood vessels don't have enough blood supply, due to inadequate blood pressure, then the brain cells at the farthest ends of the blood vessels are especially prone to death.

3. Hemorrhagic or Ischemic stroke.
This is a stroke caused either by an eruption of blood vessels or by an occlusion due to blood clots in the brain. It is important to realize that not only our brain can have a stroke. Kidneys and intestines can also have a hemorrhagic or ischemic stroke! However, when other organs have strokes, we may not realize that it is a stroke right away. Instead, we may feel unwell due to unknown reasons.

Cerebrovascular Accident
Looking from the brain blood vessels' perspective,

there are two types of strokes. Strokes may be caused by either a blockage or a breakage in a blood vessel, both leading to cell decay. Without the proper supply of blood, brain cells are deprived of oxygen, causing those cells to die. Which part of the brain will be damaged depends on the location of the affected blood vessels. Different areas of the brain are responsible for different functions. The area of the brain in which a stroke happens will determine what a patient experiences after the stroke. For example, patients who suffer a stroke on the left side of the brain will have impairment of their right arm and leg. This might lead to having difficulties eating and/or walking normally.

Blockage of blood vessels can be caused by blood clots which can be formed locally (thrombosis following atherosclerosis) or can have a different origin (embolism). For example, myocardial or valvular heart diseases or cardiac arrhythmia may cause stagnation of blood, leading to the blood thickening and forming clots. A clot may pass through bigger blood vessels but might get stuck when it reaches smaller vessels in the brain, causing ischemia, or a lack of blood, downstream. Therefore, blood clots are closely related to atherosclerosis or valvular disease.

For example, if a person doing drugs does not pay attention to sterilizing the needle, the bacteria from the unsterilized needle will reach the heart at the same time as the drug. Valves in the heart will become inflamed, and the bacteria will attach to the valve or endocardium as a parasite. This will lead to endocarditis. Once the inflammation reaches a certain point, the parasite will detach and flow through the vessels. A stroke happens once this parasite reaches the brain, causes a blockage, and forms a clot in the brain's blood vessels.

What is scary about a stroke is that it may happen suddenly. You are just fine one moment, and then all of a sudden you will lose your sight if a stroke happens in your visual cortex. If the stroke happens in the olfactory cortex, you will lose your sense of smell. If the stroke happens in the motor cortex, you will lose voluntary muscle function in a part of your body. This is usually referred to as paralysis.

A Stroke is a Torment for Both the Body and the Mind

The impact of a stroke is not limited to paralysis and/ or the loss of bodily functions. It can be a physical and a mental torment for the patient and the family. Many experts believe that a stroke puts the overall well-being of the human at risk. It is a great burden to take care of a stroke patient, who can enter a permanent vegetative state in cases of a severe stroke. Paralyzed stroke patients can develop bedsores, and this requires extra efforts on the part of the caregiver.

The feeling of inferiority, rather than the inconvenience of the body, is the most difficult issue for a stroke patient. They are worried about the residual defects after the stroke. If the brain's language center is damaged, a patient cannot speak clearly. At times they may have facial palsy due to their inability to control their facial nerves. These patients cannot look at themselves in the mirror, let alone coping with being seen by other people. They hide at home all day. After a stroke, we have to face not only issues related to the body, but even more so the mental effects. According to medical research, almost all stroke patients are depressed.

Some people believe that having a stroke is more horrible than having cancer. Other people cannot tell that you have cancer, but with a stroke, you may be confined to a wheelchair or have to walk with a walker. These more obvious symptoms can be more damaging to a person's self esteem. If they have the choice, many people would prefer a sudden death of subarachnoid hemorrhage (SAH), because they consider a quick death to be a blessing. Subarachnoid hemorrhage will not cause paralysis, and the person suffering this will die soon after a severe headache. The burst blood vessels happen in the subarachnoid, an area between the brain and the thin membrane that covers the brain, and not in the brain itself. It will not cause normal stroke symptoms, and the death rate is high. But rest assured that most headaches are not related to this.

Stroke and High Blood Pressure are not Absolutely Related

If a hemorrhagic stroke is solely caused by high blood pressure via atherosclerosis or if coronary artery disease is also solely caused by high blood pressure, then as long as we can control blood pressure, no one would ever have a stroke! But this is far away from the truth!

We believe, based on today's medical knowledge, that the older we get, the more hardened and the more fragile our arterial vessels (i.e. arteries) become. A person's blood pressure can be raised when they are enraged. If the arteries cannot bear the pressure, they will rupture. Most of the time, the arteries that rupture are the arterial vessels that are the smallest in diameter (i.e. arterioles). It is usually okay if a venous vessel (i.e. veins) ruptures, as the blood will find another path. However, if an artery ruptures, then the areas that that particular artery is responsible for serving will be affected. An artery with hardened walls has lost its elasticity. As a result it can not adapt adequately to raised blood pressure and, therefore, is at risk of rupture. As you can see, it is not high blood pressure that causes a stroke; it is because arteries lose their elasticity.

For example, a good pipe can stand a lot of pressure due to its elastic quality. Our heart pumps out blood into arteries that expand and contract as the blood flows through them. It creates the beats of our pulses. Therefore, the main cause of cardiovascular disease is due to the loss of elasticity of the arteries and not just to high blood pressure.

Take the tap water in Taipei, for example. The water is of drinkable quality at the water company. However, when the water travels through the water pipes and then reaches individual households, we can no longer drink it directly, because many of the pipes are outdated and contaminated. Similarly, we must have this understanding: High blood pressure is only a symptom and a phenomenon, not a disease! Therefore, focusing solely on controlling blood pressure will not do much good in preventing strokes. On the contrary, low blood pressure might give rise to depression. Blood pressure is a form of energy. If we cause our blood pressure to be too low in an effort to prevent strokes, we may lose our energy as well.

High blood pressure means that this person has issues from his heart all the way through his entire circulatory system. We should examine the entire circulatory system rather than focusing only on reducing blood pressure. Western treatments often are piecemeal, treating each symptom only according to the organ in which the symptom manifests itself without the holistic view of the entire body. This fruitless approach is like seeking a hare in a hen's nest and is more of a loss than a gain. Western treatments repress symptoms, but they fail to see the root cause of the problem.

To Label a Person with a Disease Will Condition That Person to Believe It Is So

My mother is about 70 years old. Recently, she had her blood pressure measured at a nearby clinic. As soon as the doctor saw the numbers, he announced to my mother, "You have high blood pressure and will need to take medicine for the rest of your life." The doctor wrote her a prescription for a month's supply of blood pressure pills. Upon hearing this, I told my mother, "You do not have high blood pressure! Your blood pressure is just temporarily a little high."

Saying, "Your blood pressure is just temporarily a little high," begins to hypnotize my mother. It implies that the blood pressure is high right now, but it does not mean this situation will continue. My mother is more at ease after hearing my statement. I then ask her, "Did you sleep well last night? Maybe you have overworked yourself a little recently? Are you a little under the weather?" She thinks for a moment and says that it is true that she has been a little more tired recently, hasn't slept well, and maybe has caught the flu.

"That's right! You do not have high blood pressure. Let's try this. Try to get a good night's sleep in the next few days. Do some exercises. When you are recovered from the flu, I will take your blood pressure reading again. If you are still concerned, then you can take one pill so you will feel at ease." A few days later, my mother's blood pressure reading has lowered as I expected. I am happy about the outcome and reaffirm to my mother, "You see! You do not have high blood pressure."

I am sure you have mixed feelings right now. If my mother had not accepted my "alternative" suggestion, she might have been on her way to lifelong medication. Her body was labeled as having high blood pressure. This story also illustrates the possibility that because of temporary high blood pressure, many people may have been taking lifelong medication for no reason. The medical term for high blood pressure is hypertension. Some patients are prone to "white coat" hypertension or "nervousness" hypertension. This can occur when a patient, seeing a doctor or a nurse wearing a white coat and carrying a blood pressure monitor, becomes nervous. As a result, the blood pressure reading may appear high. But this is only a temporary phenomenon and does not require that the patient take medication.

To label a person with a certain disease will condition that person to believe that it is so. If you feel any discomfort, do not panic and do not think that you must have a cold or high blood pressure. You must treat all diseases as a phenomenon. I get sick, too, with a fever or diarrhea, and this is how I always get myself back to health. As soon as we put a disease name to our discomfort, we believe it to be true, and our body will react accordingly. For example, if a kid has already been labeled as a "bad kid," then most likely he or she will turn out to be one. If they are already treated as if they are "bad," then what is the point of being "good?" The same principle applies to diseases.

Instead of suppressing the symptoms, the holistic approach redirects energy into creative expression. Our body, mind and spirit are designed to be extremely elastic. Whether it is hypertension or stroke, the cause is not simply due to elevated blood pressure. Instead, it is because a person's overall body system has lost its elasticity. Stroke may be, but is not absolutely, related to the amount of salt, sugar, and fat in one's diet. I often say, "You do not have high blood pressure. Even if you do, you can fix it."

Diet Control Due to Fear

The first step in the evaluation of possible cardiovascular diseases usually consists of blood tests. After reviewing the test results, a doctor might tell you, "Your cholesterol is too high. You should consider taking medicine if the number goes above 240. Your triglyceride level is also too high." In stroke prevention, the medical field stresses the importance of strict control of a person's blood pressure, more frequent exercise, and less salt in the diet to prevent hypertension. As a result, we are told to change from regular salt to low sodium salt, to increase our exercises, to eat less fatty foods, and to avoid using animal fats when cooking.

Many people are concerned about their parents' health and often watch over their parents' dietary habits. Often, adult children remind their parents again and again, "You cannot eat this; you cannot take that; you will get high blood pressure, high blood sugar, or even cancer if you eat it." Little do we know that we are giving negative hypnotic instructions to our parents, even though the original intent is love and care. Day in and day out, our parents live in fear of being sick. Oftentimes, frictions occur between the children and the parents. Parents are being restricted and threatened by invisible fear. What is there to live for if we cannot even have a good meal?

The medical profession has a long history of why and how it came to be where it is today. However, most medical information that the general public receives is superficial. For example, Finland once conducted the following experiment. Researchers put subjects into three groups: strict diet control, mild diet control, and no diet control. The research found that the subjects in the strictest diet group had the highest percentage of deaths due to a cardiovascular disease.

Why? You find no meaning to your life when you live with strict diet control. How much fun is left if everything is off-limits? The stricter they controlled their diets, the stronger the fear energy was. They had a lot of fear regarding how their food intake might adversely affect their health. Happy people live a long life. The more attention we pay to strict diet control and disease prevention, the less we are able to live our lives. Fear strongly damages our bodies and our minds, much more so than the effect of a bad diet.

Lost Faith in Health is the Killing Blow

The most threatening factor to our health is a loss of faith in our own well-being and a loss of the belief that we are healthy. It is not pesticides, air pollution, chemicals, or any other cancer-causing substances. We all know that if we lose faith in a marriage, the marriage will eventually fail. If we lose faith in a business, it will not succeed. If we lose faith in life, we will not continue to live. Therefore, we must learn the holistic approach to health! We must regain faith in our own health and the belief that we are healthy.

Eradicate all doubts about our own health; this

is the best prevention. If we lose faith in our own health, our immune system will breakdown, causing diseases to appear. No medical treatment will work when that happens. Therefore, the secret to health is to reclaim the faith and trust in our own bodies.

I believe that many cancer patients die because of their fear of cancer; they do not die because of cancer itself. Some die right away after the diagnosis while others, who are less pessimistic, live a few more years before passing. As soon as we are diagnosed with a disease, we lose faith in our health right away, and our body goes downhill from there. Interestingly, many people who have lost faith in their own bodies seem rather confident in their doctors and in medicine. However, doctors and medicine are external, something outside of ourselves. Real strength has to come from within. If our faith is based on external things such as a doctor or medicines, then as soon as a patient becomes skeptical toward their doctor or the medicine they are taking, or if they are told that there is no cure, then we can do nothing but await sentencing by the disease.

Why is SARS (Severe Acute Respiratory Syndrome) so frightening? What scares us is not the virus itself, but that we are at a loss for what to do. It is the breakdown of our faith in medicine. In the past, smallpox was an alarming disease. We have a cure now, so it is no longer so terrifying. However, the most frightening of all is that we cannot establish faith in our own bodies, nor can we put our faith in medicines.

As long as we have faith in life, even if medicine disappoints us, we can still rebuild our own mental and physical health. With faith, our health is within reach. We can lose faith in external gods, buddhas, and medicines, but we cannot lose faith in our inner self, inner vitality. This is our original energy.

I like to deepen everyone's faith, not in medicines, but in ourselves. Trust that our bodies are naturally born to have self-healing powers. We must learn how to activate this power. Instead of relying only on external medical treatments to regain health, we must trust that our bodies have undeveloped wisdom and potential. We must establish such a concept regarding our health. In the case when we are unable to get help from anyone else, we will not have a panic attack.

I have a patient who discovered unexpectedly through a routine checkup that he was already at the terminal stage of lung cancer. The doctor told him he had only three months to live. Two years have since passed, and he is still alive and well. When he went back for a checkup, the cancer was gone! The path of spiritual growth helps us to rediscover the old wisdom of our own bodies, and it teaches us not to rely only on external technology. No one can help a person who has lost faith in his or her own vitality.

Inflexible Thinking Will Harden Blood Vessels

A fifty-something year old single female suddenly has a stroke. A relative suggests that she come to see me and then tells me that the stroke victim runs a hardware store by herself and has a bad temper. What surprises me is that she has no history of high blood pressure. Traditionally, a stroke patient usually has a history of high blood pressure and would be taking long-term medication.

"Are you a person with a short temper? Do you dislike even a short wait on anything?" I usually ask these kinds of questions to this type of patient. "Do you frequently throw temper tantrums? Do you always demand that others follow your orders? And when other people do not listen to you, do you get angry?" Usually patients acknowledge these statements. Common characteristics among people with high blood pressure and stroke are a short temper and that they get mad easily.

Humans are run by the so-called autonomic nervous system which controls the entire cardiovascular system. There are factors that effect the cardiovascular system in the long term and other factors in the short term. According to the medical field, those factors that have adverse effects in the long term include high cholesterol, high triglycerides, high blood pressure, hardening of arterial walls, blockage of arteries, etc. According to the body-mind-spirit philosophy, however, the causes are not that simple. The truth lies in the fact that as people grow old, they lose more and more sources of happiness and flexibility.

If a person's thinking has no flexibility, if he lives a routine daily life—gets up in the morning, goes to work, eats food, and sleeps—where everything follows a prescribed pattern, then this is a stubborn person without much room for growth in life. As soon as we become stubborn, our blood vessels become hardened. Blood vessels' elasticity represents a person's elasticity or flexibility within his own life. Being elastic is like a balloon full of air. If you drop the balloon, it bounces back. A person without flexibility will not be adaptable when facing different situations. This person is usually quick tempered, must handle everything immediately, might have insomnia due to an overactive autonomic nervous system, and is more subject to cardiovascular diseases. The older they get, the more stubborn they might become.

Cardiovascular diseases are issues of the entire body system. Fixing them with a bypass operation or by a stent placement alone will not solve the root cause of the issue. Take the bypass operation, for example. When your coronary arteries are blocked, your doctor may treat the problem by removing or redirecting blood vessels from one area of the body and placing them around the narrowed area to "bypass" the block-ages and restore blood flow to the heart muscle. It is like creating a bypass of a congested highway. If the traffic issue is not solved fundamentally, building more bypasses will not alleviate the issue. The holistic ap-proach we are learning aims to change our health sys-tem from the inside out.

At times, some long-term factors cause cardiovas-cular diseases, including hardening or narrowing of the arteries. A good analogy is a rubber band. A rubber band, when new, is elastic. But it will become fatigued, lose its elasticity, and break easily, if it has been stretched for too long. The water hose in the garden will harden and easily break after having been exposed to sunlight for too long. Our blood vessels are the same. However, our blood vessels are neither rubber bands nor water hoses; our blood vessels can adapt. As we get older, it is not a given that our blood vessels will become fragile and lose their elasticity. This is an im-portant holistic concept for our health. Through prac-tice and a transformation of our thought patterns, our body will change accordingly. In short, regardless of our actual age, if we can keep a child-like heart, we can keep our vitality charging. Our body energy comes from our inner vitality, in the same way that running water is full of energy. If our body energy continues to flow freely, how can we have a stroke or hypertension?

Let Vitality Flow Like Running Water

Fresh running water will have fish, while stagnated water will not. If we let our vitality flow as freely as running water, then our entire physical body system, from heart to blood vessels, will be vibrant. Then high cholesterol and triglyceride levels will no longer be a threat, as we understand that the real key lies in living a flexible life. Many people become more and more unhappy because their vitality has stopped flowing. I am over forty years old and still full of energy and passion. I believe I will be the same even in my seventies. Life should have new stimuli, just as water should be allowed to run freely. If we are full of vitality, our bodies will function normally.

Small changes in routine daily life create a different life energy and can improve long-term cardiovascular issues and problems with aging blood vessels. We can live to a very old age and still be healthy. What is most important is to live and learn.

 **with Dr. Hsu**

Question: What can I do when I have already been diagnosed with high blood pressure and am taking medicine regularly?

Response: First of all, get rid of the idea that you have to take high blood pressure medicine for the rest of your life. You must believe that you can reverse high blood pressure. If you do want to reverse it, you must face the disease, accepting it as a phenomenon. Think of this disease as a black cloud passing through and bringing rain. Yet you know that the rain will not last for the rest of your life.

Our body is elastic and can self-heal. Changing one's diet, doing exercises, and taking medicine will not solve the root cause of the problem. We must begin to adjust our lifestyle, to change our worldview, and to see the future differently. We should treat having high blood pressure as a phenomenon. Since all phenomena can be changed, so can high blood pressure.

In addition, you must find out what has been bothering you. The short-term treatment goal is to ease anxiety. The long-term treatment goal is for a complete transformation of attitude and lifestyle. Be a child again. Get away from your rigid lifestyle. Grow through learning new things. All diseases can be healed if you start doing these things.

The path to spiritual growth will bring many inconceivable happenings. Of course, unimaginable vitality comes through from our inner self with a potential that is not yet recognized and discovered. We must have faith in regaining our health. Such a faith will help reduce anxiety and relieve problems associated with an overactive autonomic nervous system. Once we are at peace, life will begin to open up and allow us to see more possibilities.

➤ Reminder from Dr. Hsu

If you have hypertension or have had a stroke, you must ask yourself a very personal question. Have you accumulated a lot of repression, compromise, or anger either at work or with people in significant relationships, such as your children or your parents? For example, maybe you have a spouse with a strong personality who holds a better job with a higher income than you do. You consistently have to repress your anger and unhappiness. By doing so, on the surface you seem to have avoided many conflicts. However, you have accumulated a lot of anger, fear, and helplessness inside yourself that you feel you cannot express outwardly. You must begin to face and release these accumulated negative energies, as they are the real causes of your disease.

Chapter 3
Heart Attack: Soften Your Heart

Western medicine believes that heart diseases are caused by arterial issues. From the holistic perspective, heart diseases are due to stagnated "heart energy." People with heart diseases are usually unhappy about things: dislike this, unhappy about that. When a person's life vitality is not open and not flowing, no medical treatment can cure heart diseases. Because the real key in curing heart diseases lies in the vitality of one's heart.

Heart Palpitation is not a Heart Disease

Many people have the experience of heart palpitations where you suddenly feel your heart is skipping beats, fluttering, beating too fast, or pumping harder than usual. Many might think they have a heart disease. As a matter of fact, there are many reasons that might cause a palpitation such as skipping breakfast, having an empty stomach for too long, drinking too much caffeine or alcohol, suddenly stopping medicine that you have been taking for a long period of time, or suddenly stopping drinking when you are used to drinking. However, palpitations will not raise your blood pressure; it will only make you feel uncomfortable.

I have experienced heart palpitations myself. It

happened one day in my clinic. I had to catch a 2 o'clock flight to Hong Kong. There were five more patients waiting to see me, but it was already twelve o'clock. I worried that I was going to be late. I became anxious, and my heart began to pump faster than usual. Many people experience heart palpitations in a similar situation. Maybe they are on their way to take an important examination but are stuck in traffic. Maybe they are in a hurry to turn in an important report, but their computer breaks down. Usually you are in a time-sensitive situation, yet you are delayed due to some circumstance. You are unable to solve the issue at the moment, so heart palpitations might happen in this case.

Usually we do not particularly notice how our heart beats, unless we take our pulse, use a stethoscope, or use our arms as a pillow. If you are just sitting still and all of a sudden feel the beating of your heart, then you might have a heart palpitation. This is not a heart disease and is usually related to stress, anxiety, overexcitement, or unbalanced emotions. Many panic disorder patients will go see a cardiologist who usually will not find any problem. The most they might find is mild mitral valve prolapse (MVP). This is because when a palpitation occurs, we cannot tell whether it is due to the normal workings of the sympathetic nervous system or to a heart disease.

Most of the time, when we feel our hearts pump harder or faster than usual, it is not due to the issue of the heart itself. Rather, the heart might be under the influence of our autonomic nervous system (ANS). The sympathetic part of the ANS makes our heart beat faster, while the parasympathetic part of the ANS reduces our heart beat. However, the ANS in our stomach functions the opposite way. For example, when you are in a race, your heart must pump faster, while your digestive functions should be lowered. Our body magically knows how to balance itself; when our nervous system is excited or stimulated, our body knows which functions to enhance and which functions to weaken. When the sympathetic ANS is working, our blood pressure will be raised and our pupils dilated. We are in a state of excitement and action.

As you can see, many times palpitations are caused by internal stimuli, such as overworking, too much stress or anxiety, always running behind schedule, or the accumulation of fearful energy in our subconsciousness. We work ourselves up so much during the day that we might not be able to sleep at night as we are still overstimulated. Some women might even experience palpitations before their period comes.

Reclaim Our Body's Own Healing Power, Starting with not Relying on Medications

Some people worry that they might become too nervous during important moments, so they take anti-anxiety drugs to tranquilize/relax their nerves. From the holistic perspective, however, we can only reclaim our body's own ability/power when we learn not to rely on medication. Seth teaches us that our bodies are born to be healthy. Diseases are here only for educational purposes. Only when we are sick, do we dare to call a timeout and to examine our lives. Diseases allow us to see the repressed self inside. If we rely on medication to lessen the condition, we miss our golden opportunity to look inside, to see ourselves through our diseases. It is very difficult to really cure the root of the disease this way.

I am not saying use no medication at all. However, we must remember this concept: The less medication we take, the healthier we are. Physiologically speaking, too much medication will interfere with our body's natural balance, especially during the process of a natural death. A natural death occurs when our body and organs have deteriorated to the point that our soul and physical body naturally separate. I always suggest using as little medication as possible, when facing sickness or even multiple organ failure. If you observe carefully, you will see that in a hospital a patient who is taking a large amount of medication will usually continue to live though suffering and unable to move forward towards death. Alternatively, with less medication, the separation of the soul and the body will happen naturally.

When our soul and body integrate, they sign a contract. They agree that when the body is at the end of its time on earth, it will end its contract with the soul. If the contract ends smoothly, then the soul, being blessed, will leave the body joyfully. This is such a blessing for the terminally ill. However, medication will interfere with this natural process, resulting in a difficult separation of the soul from the body. On the surface, it might appear that the patient suffers less. The truth is, it is a torture. So I often say this: The less medication a person takes in his or her life, the smoother the death process will be. When the end of our physical time on earth has come, all we want is a "good death."

I often like to make this analogy. If, every time a child encounters a challenge, the parent immediately solves the problem for the child, then this child will never have the chance to cultivate his or her own problem-solving abilities. The same principle applies to our body's health. If we always turn to medication when we are sick, then our body will create this dependency on medication. Our body will become weaker and weaker without having the chance to grow its own healing abilities. This is similar to people who rely on sleeping pills until they become psychologically dependent on them. A dependence on medication creates a belief that "If I don't take medication, I will not recover from my illness." Eventually this will develop into a pattern where you will turn to medication regardless of the degree of your illness.

In the past, we did not have the correct concepts about medication. We used to believe that the faster we can see their effects, the better the medication. Many doctors used to like to add steroids to a prescription. Patients would see a quick turn-around after taking one or two doses. Little did we know how damaging these drugs are to our body. We have to use stronger and stronger doses each time, creating a vicious cycle. We see the same issues in the use of antibiotics. Every time you have an infection, you take antibiotics, and your body loses its own defensive ability in the process. This is one of the reasons why when SARS swept Taiwan, many people's bodies had no ability to defend against the virus. We must recognize that the more effective a drug seems, the more damaging it is to our bodies.

Many of the elderly seem uneasy if they do not take medication even for one day. Their rooms are so full of a variety of drugs that they could even open a drug store! How can we have a happy life without our health? Therefore, we must begin to grow holistically, integrating body, mind and spirit. We must understand that when our body is in a balanced state, immunity and healing powers will happen naturally. We must get rid of the idea that we should take medication to recover from an illness. Instead, when we catch the flu from which it might take someone else one to two weeks to recover, it will take us only one to two days to see improvement. And this can be accomplished without taking any medication! Give this a try! Start now. To stimulate your body's potential power, learn not to resort to medication. Allow your body the opportunity to develop its self-healing abilities!

Healing Must Start From Opening Up One's Energy Flow

While there are many kinds of heart disease, coronary artery disease is the most common type. The heart is composed of muscles which function like a pump, sending oxygen and blood to organs throughout the body. However, the heart cells cannot get nutrition directly. They get oxygen and nutrition from the coronary arteries that branch off of the main artery of the body called the aorta. When these coronary arteries are narrowed or obstructed, the heart muscles will become damaged. This kind of heart disease is called coronary artery disease.

There are many causes for coronary artery disease, such as atherosclerosis (or arteriosclerosis), coronary artery spasm, thrombosis or stenosis. By the way, coronary artery spasm is not a real heart disease. Some particularly sensitive people experience a sensation of oxygen deprivation when their arteries contract, mimicking symptoms of a heart attack.

The symptoms of a heart attack include cold hands, cold feet, sweating, chest pain as if the heart is bundled up by a rope. Because of the anatomy of the body and the nervous system, at times people might experience soreness in their shoulders. Many people with depression may also experience heaviness across the chest, as if a big boulder lays on the chest. They may also feel cold and sweaty, but this is not quite the same as an actual acute heart attack.

Arteriosclerosis causes the thickening and hardening of the walls of the three coronary arteries. Due to the accumulation of debris, the blood flow is compromised. When under stress or after heavy exercise or a big meal, a person feels discomfort in the chest, then this is caused by a lack of oxygen in the heart muscles, possibly leading to the onset of a heart attack. In this instance, a nitroglycerin tablet placed under the tongue will dilate the arteries and thus increase the blood flow to the heart muscles.

Here is an interesting analogy. Do you know how to put out a fire on an oil rig? You set up explosives, which will quickly consume all the oxygen in the air and, therefore, put out the fire. This is how the drug nitroglycerin works, as an "explosive" to help dilate the blood vessels. Many people with heart problems are quick-tempered and have an explosive personality. Using nitroglycerin is like finding an even more explosive element to fight against this person. Every time I think about this analogy, I cannot help but feel amazed by the magic of our bodies.

Western medicine believes that heart diseases are caused by arterial issues. From the holistic perspective, heart diseases are due to stagnated "heart energy." These people are usually unhappy about things: dislike this, unhappy about that. When a person's life vitality is not open and not flowing, no medical treatment can cure heart diseases. Because the real key in curing heart diseases lies in one's heart's vitality. I often quote Seth, "... a man who feels that he has no heart will not be saved by the most sophisticated heart transplant." In order to cure a heart problem, we must first find out where this person's vitality is repressed.

Current Western medicine treats coronary artery diseases by using medication, an interventional treatment (stent implantation procedure to widen the arteries), surgery (coronary artery bypass graft surgery), or diet control. Propaganda focuses on "eating a less fatty diet," because many believe that too much cholesterol and too many triglycerides will increase the chances of a blood vessel blockage. From the holistic perspective, however, all these methods will not be able to solve the root of the problem. Disappointment and sadness are the two main causes of a heart problem. Heart is the source of energy. When the heart itself loses its vitality, the person will, too. Similarly, if we are happy, our metabolism will function well.

Cholesterol, triglycerides, and blood pressure will be taken care of by our bodies. There is no need to be concerned about watching our diet. The true prevention is to teach people how to live happily instead of thinking that our lives are heavy burdens.

Simply Do What You Can / Be Happy with What You Can Do

A patient comes to see me. He has high cholesterol and is taking medication to lower it. This kind of medication damages the liver, so he is conflicted. Furthermore, what bothers him the most is the fact that he has been a vegetarian for years, exercises regularly, and practices Buddhist meditation daily. How can he have high cholesterol? I ask him about any recent changes in his life. He shares that his father passed away recently and left him with a Buddhist monastery to manage.

Since then, two abbots had come and gone due to ir-reconcilable differences involving how they like to run a monastery. The entire situation was unhappy, and everything was a tremendous mess. He ended up tak-ing over the monastery himself, but he is on the verge of a breakdown. Taking care of day-to-day details in a monastery has become a huge burden!

In the old days when people had malnutrition, cholesterol was desirable because only nutritious food was high in cholesterol. Interestingly, the majority of cholesterol is not taken in through food, but it is pro-duced through our liver. Fat is the main element of our cell membranes, and the main function of a membrane is to protect a cell from its surroundings. If we do not have enough fat to have strong cell membranes, we are more prone to cancer. Physiologically speaking, cho-lesterol is a form of high-energy sources. Why would too much of this kind of energy accumulate in the body? The answer is clear from the holistic perspective. In this patient's case, his cholesterol had been normal. It only began to rise with the recent events regarding the monastery. These things created stress, on top of his already busy work life. He has too many things to worry about, and his life vitality has become stagnated.

I advise him that all religious activities bring peo-ple peace of mind. I tell him, "When you walk into your Buddhist monastery, you should bring this attitude with you: No matter what I do, it is good enough. Whether you decide to put the flowers to the right or to the left side of the statue, the Buddha will not be mad at you. Nor will you be punished if you schedule a wrong day for the offering ceremony. If the more we practice Buddhism, the more we become uneasy about the details of the ceremony, then we are doing this wrong." Many people are not practicing Buddhism but are practicing "asking-for-trouble." When we are bound by precepts or cause-and-effect, we might end up becoming psycho and losing sight of the true meaning of the practice. Being relaxed and not bound by official social norms are the keys to enlightenment.

When did it become a burden simply to live? It is not our body or our food that has caused burdensome sickness. The burdensome feeling starts in our minds and then shows up in our bodies. For example, a coworker gives you a task that you do not want to do. Yet, you do not know how to say no. As a result, you complain while working on the task. In the meantime, you wonder why you are so fed up. It feels as if the entire world is against you! Every morning you wake up and think about the meetings you have to go to, the progress you have to make, the house cleaning you have to do, and the meals you have to cook. When day in and day out, all we feel is stress and not how we can live our passion, then our mind becomes burdened, and we are not happy.

I helped this patient to understand that his high cholesterol is not directly related to his diet or exercise but his state of mind. I also suggested to him that he start doing things that make him happy! Do things that you really want to do, rather than things that you are obligated to do. As to the monastery, he could sell it or hire a management company to take care of running it. When he retires from his day job, he could also consider taking it over at that point. The key is to handle this process as something that is fun. If the face of the Buddha statue gets dirty, he can clean it up. If he wants a vacation, then he should ask for days off from Buddha and be on his way!

In Yi Jing, (also know as the I Ching), the Chinese Classic Book of Change, there is a phrase "*Dong Ze De Jiu*" meaning "each decision comes with potential good and bad consequences." An even deeper meaning behind this concept is this: We must face the challenges and risks inherent in each task, and we learn our life lessons this way. There are always two sides to every coin, and we can decide on which side to focus. For example, many grandpas and grandmas are troubled by their naughty grandchildren and come to my clinic seeking help. I always tell them, grandchildren are here for you to laugh with and play with, not for you to worry about. Your role as a grandparent is to enjoy your time with your grandchildren. Leave the responsibility of educating them to their parents.

We always have too high an expectation towards life, career or our children. For heart disease patients, the higher the expectation, the more the disappointment. Sadness, discouragement, and the desire to quit stagnate our heart's vitality. It is then that our cholesterol levels and our triglyceride levels begin to damage our hearts and block our blood vessels. All religions are meant to bring joy to people. Even if we do not do a perfect job, as long as we learn from our mistakes, then there is no need to blame ourselves or to worry about punishment due to cause and effect. This is the way to practice. When facing any task, we should tell ourselves that we will simply do what we can, enjoying the process and being happy with whatever results we get. Then we can release any burden from of our mind.

Learn to Let Go and to Soften Your Heart

Seth mentions that many people with heart problems are people without peace of mind. Indeed, too many things can bother us. Why are males more inclined to have heart problems? There is a joke that goes like this: A child calls home and says, "Hello, Dad. Is Mom home?" Dad becomes the operator; the child always asks for Mom instead of him. Many males are lonely inside. He seldom communicates with his wife, and he easily gets mad at his children. He always feels that no one wants to talk to him without realizing what a bad-tempered person he is. He is the one who does not want to talk to anyone and who appears distant. Living such a lonely life, he suffers inside. A lonely heart brings on heart problems.

Our heart is the first to reflect our inner feelings among all organs. By the same token, how we feel impacts our heart's health. If we want a healthy heart, we must open our heart's vitality. Once our heart's energy is flowing, it can then receive energy from our body, mind and spirit. From our heart muscles to our blood pressure, our arteries and our veins, all parts of our circulatory system will be healthy. Our blood vessels are not only the passage for flowing blood but also the channel for expressing our feelings. Our feelings are as rich as the blood circulating in our bodies. But when such a vibrant energy is blocked due to worries and helplessness, our body energy is affected as well.

Many people with anemia are not really deficient in red blood cells, but they lack the force of life vitality. Many people suffer from dizziness, because they feel powerless in their lives. This is why exercise can build muscles and help improve anemia. Exercise is a form of power similar to yelling or screaming. From this perspective, when what is flowing in the arteries lacks in feelings and love, the blood vessels are blocked. This person lacks love energy in his life and may feel very lonely.

Seth suggests that people with heart problems should have a pet. Everyday you should comb its fur, walk with it, and play with it. More and more reports have come out suggesting that a pet's presence is beneficial to a person's health. Through the interaction with a pet, your feelings begin to flow. It gives you a warm fuzzy feeling that a person and a pet can accompany each other and take care of each other. When we are touched, our feelings will flow better and so will our blood. For example, it is said that dogs are man's best friends. We might be disappointed with our spouse, discouraged by our children, or even giving up on ourselves. But our beloved dog will never give up on his master! We can smile or cry or even tell secrets to them without the worry of betrayal. He will always wag his tail and respond with his warm loyal eyes. For heart patients, having a pet is a more effective treatment than any kind of medicine or surgery. A pet can soften our hearts and help our feelings to flow again.

Seth teaches us that if we can find the belief and attitude behind each disease, then we can change our beliefs and adjust our attitudes. Our feelings and our energy will instantly be opened up. When we feel sunny, we walk with lightness. With the same body, however, when we suffer with pains and burdens, each step weighs a thousand pounds. Our heart beats 24 hours, seven days a week without a break; it promises us a healthy body until old age. Nevertheless, we are repaying it with heavy shackles that make it out of breath. This is the main reason of heart issues.

Let me give you an analogy. Imagine a hot air balloon with sandbags hanging around it. When we release the sandbags, the hot air balloon will move up into the sky. Suppose the balloon wants to go up, but the sandbags are holding it down. Once the fuel is burned up, the balloon will collapse. Sandbags are hindrances, with each bag having a name: worry about public safety, fear for our children's future, financial concerns about retirement, etc. Countless sandbags strangle our heart until it fails. Our heart problems come from worrying about this, that, and all of the other things that have not yet happened. Will worry solve our problems? No! Worry will only burden our hearts!

Learning about the holistic perspective of body, mind and spirit will help you to let go of one sandbag at a time. My child cannot get a divorce. As long as the two people know what they want, so be it. My company is going downhill. Will constant complaints and worry solve anything? Either I find another job, or I need to find joy at the current job among the chaos. Life should be joyful, and events occur in order for us to learn something. Do not make life a burden. If we can release the sandbags from the hot air balloon, without any surgery even a middle-aged heart patient can regain the health of a very young person's heart. In the holistic practice, the most powerful energy is love. When we can open ourselves up and begin to interact with others, our hearts will begin to flow with an unlimited supply of vitality.

Changing Our Mind is Better Than Acting Out

Let me give you an example. Let's say I have a daughter for whom I have expectations. I know what major I want her to pursue in college, where I want her to work, and what kind of person I want her to marry. She does not appreciate my suggestions and wants to marry someone of whom I disapprove. My heart is chilled facing my beloved daughter's decision. Shortly after that, I am diagnosed with a heart problem that requires surgery.

Many people have experienced similar scenarios without realizing the true cause of their heart issue. They focus only on "I love my children. I wish them to be happy, but they do not listen." I often ask, "In the name of love, do we prefer them to follow the path that we have planned for them or to follow the path on which their hearts have led them?" Ultimately, we want our children to be happy. We often mistake love for expectation. I love you, so you must follow my words, as what I say is for your own good. To plan ahead for them, of course, is a form of love; however, love is more than that. Love also means understanding, acceptance, respect, and allowing them the freedom to make their own decisions regarding their own lives.

I often advise parents that young people have their own ideas. As long as they are happy, no matter what they do, allow them to take the responsibility of their own decisions. Parents should not interfere too much. Of course, you would be hurt if your daughter insists on marrying someone of whom you disapprove. But do we have to throw her out and tell her never to return home? If we really decide to end this relationship, we hurt ourselves as well as our daughter. Suppose the marriage indeed fails. Then your daughter will not dare to get a divorce. She might prefer to struggle on her own instead of coming home. You and your daughter both are hurt in such a scenario.

We should learn to soften our hearts and to let go. We have the option to tell our daughter, "Even though I do not like this guy you wish to marry, you still have my blessings. In case one day you are not happy in this marriage, you can always come home. I am always here for you." Keep a light on for her and allow her the leeway to come home. This is the best support we can offer. We should never act out in anger.

The more we love them, the more we should learn to let go. Yielding is not a weakness. To yield does not mean that I am less than you are. It means an even bigger love, respect, and tolerance.

I was once rebellious and made my mom cry. I was in puberty and full of self-righteousness. I argued with her and made her hide in her room while she cried. I later knelt down outside her door, apologizing, "Mom, I am sorry. I did not mean to hurt you." Let's yield for love. Yielding requires even more courage and strength than remaining rigid. Suppose your spouse has an affair. Even though you are full of anger, do not act out in anger and do things that hurt both of you. Soften your heart; yield to love. This is wise, as nothing is more powerful than love.

Our previous President Lee (of Taiwan) has blockages in his blood vessels and has had over ten stent implantation procedures. To a certain degree, as a leader, he must be cold-blooded at times. However, no one likes to be such a person. When we become cold-blooded, we hurt ourselves the most. The enemies we hate the most are usually the ones about which we care the most. To have compassion toward our enemies means to have compassion toward ourselves. It is pointless to be so angry at someone else's mistakes. The same principle applies to heart diseases. Can we loosen up a little? Can we let it go?

We should live a carefree life. The older we get, the more wisdom we should gain. We should practice how to untangle ourselves from a rigid personality structure. Enjoy life rather than being confined by endless layers of rules. A patient once shared with me that she comes from a family of doctors with a certain reputation in town. She has to be very careful of everything she does in order to live up to that reputation. She lives a life filled with constraints. When she encounters a difficulty in life, she is afraid to seek help, fearing what people might think of her. You see how we are trapped by our own minds? Do things have to go in a certain way? Seth says, "You create your own reality!" This means that my life will develop according to my beliefs. The more rigid my beliefs are, the more constrained my life will be. Eventually, we will put ourselves into a corner with no way out.

When a troublesome thought occurs, ask yourself, "Do I have to think this way? Are there any other perspectives?" When a thought is changed, we might feel as free as if the sky were the limit! The more open our thoughts are, the more open our mind becomes. When we encounter difficulties in life, remember the following two principles:

1. Allow love to flow. Cry if you feel like crying. Allow your emotions to flow and express how you truly feel inside.

2. Let go of all worries and hindrances in life.

Many conflicts arise when both sides insist on their own point of view. Like letting go, one at a time, the sandbags on the hot air balloon, the holistic practice encourages us to let go of worries, readjust life goals, and fly free. When we reach this state of mind, we will be healthier as we get older, and we will have a new perspective about life.

 with Dr. Hsu

Question: Why do elderly males commonly have prostate issues?

Response: Prostate issues represent the loss of self-esteem as males grow older. If a man cannot adapt and readjust to a different stage of life, then he may get prostate hyperplasia or prostate cancer.

A prostate cancer patient tells me how he was on top of the world before his retirement, with money and social status. People tried to get closer to him, tried to create a relationship with him. All these became things of the past after retirement. However, he missed the days when he was a mover and a shaker. Every time he has an argument with his daughter, he would talk all about the glorious past. But he would always be at a loss as to what to say and became furious when his daughter fought back, saying, "All that happened a long time ago!" Similarly, many middle-or high-ranking officers have difficulty adjusting to life after retirement, because they are unable to transform themselves to a different stage of life.

Life itself changes constantly. If you are resistant to change, you get sick. Prostate issues represent the mourning of a male's lost power and status. No matter who you are, there is no exception that we seek outlets to express our life's vitality. Before retirement, we express ourselves through the outlets of career, profession, fame, and money. After retirement, we must find a different outlet. We must transform ourselves in accordance with our current stage of life. For example, after her children have grown, a stay-at-home mother should readjust her focus in life and begin to live for herself.

I tell that prostate cancer patient to begin to adjust his focus in life! Let go of social status and fame and begin to get in touch with his soul. Middle and old age are the times to develop spirituality. This is a time when we do not need any external status or fame to affirm who we are. We should begin to ask ourselves, "Why do I want to live? Where do we go after death?" This is the next stage for spiritual growth, in which we look inside ourselves and expand our holistic view on the integration of body, mind, and spirit.

➤ Reminder from Dr. Hsu

Are you in despair about life, things, and the people you care about? This kind of negative energy, if accumulated, will cause the lack of oxygen in your heart muscle and will cause your heart to fail. If you want to be cured without medication, then you must clean out this negative energy. Have a talk therapy with a psychologist or a counselor; dump out all the pains that have been buried inside. Face your life, love, family relationships, career and your future with a new heart. Becoming a "person with a heart" will allow you to reclaim the health of your heart!

Chapter 4
Diabetes: Do Not Stop Being Happy

If you are a slave to life, you will get chronic diseases. If you are free-spirited, you will live a life that is blessed with good luck all along and with plenty of time to pursue your passions. For many years I have studied the intricacies between diseases and the body, mind and spirit. For diabetes, I have gained a deep personal understanding. Many people with diabetes are dull and bored inside. They are unhappy people! You see no passion from them. They simply live day by day as if they are in a jail and chained with heavy shackles.

Diabetes is the Soul's Chronic Depression

The food that we eat is digested, absorbed, and transformed into glucose, which is a form of blood sugar. Glucose then enters into your cells through the walls of the capillaries. Next, the cells oxidize the glucose into energy for our bodies. This is the normal process. What happened that prevents blood sugars from entering into your cells? These blood sugars then stay in the blood, causing high blood sugar levels and diabetes. The typical symptoms of a person with diabetes include increased hunger, excessive thirst, frequent urination, and weight loss. Blood sugars pass through the cells, yet the cells say, "I am too lazy to process you!" This is because the cells are depressed.

Some early signs of depression include loss of appetite, lack of interest and concentration, and fatigue. When our cells are depressed, they are languid, do not want to move, do not want to eat. This is a form of chronic fatigue. Food enters into our digestive system and is transformed into blood sugar, which our cells are not interested in absorbing. These sugars have nowhere to go but to stay in our blood system. Of course, our blood sugar level then is raised.

When we are trapped in a mode of life that is not joyful, every day is unhappy. How can our body cells be happy if we are not happy? Unhappy cells naturally do not have a good appetite. Therefore, to cure diabetes, we must resolve our cells' depression and entrust our souls with their own vitality. This is the holistic approach which is the only approach that can really cure diabetes.

People with diabetes are usually unhappy people. For example, many may be blue collar workers. From the moment they open their eyes in the morning, they have to work hard, making just enough money to support their families. There is no room for leisure activities nor personal time in life. No matter how fatigued they feel, they must keep going. Depression then slowly starts to accumulate inside. When we no longer feel joy and satisfaction in life, the negative energy in our souls will create an array of diseases in modern society. There will be high levels of uric acid, cholesterol, triglycerides, and blood sugar.

When our souls cannot find creative outlets for their expression, it creates these modern diseases. However, when we do find what makes us happy, when we do have a goal to work for, then all the accumulated negative energy can be burned off. An analogy would be if we have done a hard workout and are perspiring, then we have burned off a lot of fat. However, if what awaits us everyday is a lot of "must-dos" that are not enjoyable, if we do not have life's passion to function as the fuel, then no matter how hard we work out the <u>negative energy will not be burned off</u>.

In other words, diabetes means that our cells are depressed and that we have a deep helplessness in our lives. We feel that we will live like this until we die. Diabetes can be said to be a chronic suicide!

Traditionally, society values the pursuit of external fame and money. People are valuable only if they can take on their harsh lives. We seldom are encouraged to live genuinely, to pursue what we truly love. We don't really know what kind of future to create because we are so accustomed to following the path set by our society. If we ever dare to escape these social expectations and to pursue what makes us happy, then we will suffer the "original sin of feeling happy." We simply cannot allow ourselves to relax.

So if you have diabetes, you must learn how to live happily. If diseases only make more suffering, then our souls will choose to leave this earth. The survivors of diabetes are those people who have figured out how to live a happier life than the one they had before they got sick. This is a universal law.

Many patients have told me that they are in a hurry to regain their health so they can get their lives back. I always say to them, "You are putting the cart before the horse! You are sick exactly because of your old lifestyle. If you return to the same old way of living, then you will become ill again. The holistic approach to health integrating body, mind, and spirit is the key to healing." I hope everyone clearly establishes this concept: Take the holistic approach as the principle approach, and make the medical treatments complementary.

What I am suggesting may sound unscientific. Yet it is actually the most solid approach to health. Science can only measure what it can measure. How much does one kilogram of love cost? How much does joy weigh? Does owing one kilogram of gold equal owing one kilogram of happiness? Science cannot measure these. There is only one way to solve chronic diseases. Start by changing your mode of living and by learning the holistic approach. In order to cure illness, we must work from our hearts. When our way of thinking is changed, then our diseases can be cured.

We Should Not Have Chronic Diseases

Modern medicine believes that chronic diseases, including diabetes, can only be controlled and cannot be cured. For example, every time the holiday seasons are near, nutritionists will encourage the public to control their diets and eat less greasy or fried foods. Honestly speaking, this kind of public education is not very helpful. First, the key to health is not based on our diet. Second, strict diet control requires strong will. It is inhuman that you are not allowed to eat what you see around you. In Seth's teachings, however, there is no such concept as "chronic diseases." Seth teaches that all chronic diseases can be cured.

When their blood sugar level is high, most people will first try to reduce their blood sugar. For less serious cases, doctors usually would suggest weight loss training, using diet control and exercises. However, human beings can be lazy. Plus eating nice food can be such a joyful thing. As a result, the doctor's order might be executed in fits and starts. Mainstream medicine believes that diabetes should be treated mainly with medications. If medication can control it well, a patient can live to an old age. If medication fails to control the blood sugar level, then the patient might need to receive insulin injections. Furthermore, due to pathological changes in the blood vessels and surrounding nerves, many people face amputation, blindness, or even dialysis. All these methods can only control, but not cure, diabetes. You should also know that anti-diabetes medications are harmful to our bodies.

I once had a high cholesterol patient who suffered from panic attacks because he had to take medication. On the one hand, he worried his cholesterol medication would be harmful to his liver. On the other hand, he worried that he might suffer from coronary artery disease or even a stroke if he did not take the medication. Many patients face this kind of dilemma. Take my breast cancer patient, for another example. If she continues with her treatments to prevent a breast cancer relapse, she might contract endometrial cancer. She lives daily with great anxiety. She is a vegetarian and exercises regularly. However, as long as her concern remains, any exercise, diet, or healthy philosophies will not be able to ease her worries.

The medical field is like a knife with two sides: One side cuts out diseases effectively, the other side, however, cuts ourselves. For example, when we receive chemotherapy, the tumor might be temporarily removed, yet our cells are equally harmed. The symptom might be alleviated, yet the actual damage to our body is hard to measure, not to mention the lifelong suffering from the treatments and medications. The current medical system believes that if an organ is ill, then it should be cut out. Eventually, we could cut out all of our organs. How can we be healthy using this approach? Trained in the mainstream medical system, I deeply understand the current medical field's limitations and its utmost shortcoming: The lack of an integrated holistic approach to health, which is concerned with the integrity of a patient's body, mind, and spirit.

It is not difficult to treat diseases. However, the key principle to health requires a long-term perspective and using solutions that cure. Seth teaches us that human bodies are not supposed to have chronic diseases. I deeply agree. Western medicine believes that chronic diseases cannot be cured. However, this is not true. Western medicine cannot cure them because it has not yet found the true cause of these diseases. Treatments remain at a superficial material level without the exploration of the patient's inner world. They ignore the fact that all diseases start when our "minds" are sick. Mind diseases can only be treated with mind medicines. Our bodies are a reflection of our inner world. I have never found a happy, stress-free person to be sick. Even if someone were to tell me that that is the case for him, this only means that he is deceiving himself due to his lack of awareness of his inner status.

Happiness Means Health

A patient once shared with me that he had closed his small shop a few years ago due to a decline in the economy. Since then, he had been living a life of tea drinking, chitchatting, and newspaper reading. He was very surprised a year later when he was diagnosed with diabetes, since he was only 51 years old. After retirement, he seemed to be living a carefree life. However, deep inside, he felt a helplessness toward life. Fifty one is a rather awkward age—it is not too old, but it is also not too young. He no longer has the courage to start anew. Plus, the economy was down. Yet it was really too early to retire. He was not happy about any of this and started to have symptoms of chronic depression.

Diabetes is caused by a deep helpless feeling in life. Trapped by all sorts of practical concerns, these people cannot be true to themselves, cannot be happy from the bottom of their hearts. Their souls lose energy and life direction, and their sorrow finds no way out. Maybe they appear healthy before their diagnosis. However, diabetes had started long before, when he felt no motivation and when he only felt responsibilities and pressure in life. Even if he were willing to break the pattern at his current age, he does not dare to undertake a new life chapter.

Being such a responsible person, nevertheless, his body faithfully reflects his soul's unhappiness. His soul is imprisoned with no vitality. Western medicine will tell you that diabetes is caused by an inferior quality of insulin produced by our bodies and because our cells have a lower acceptance of insulin. These are not the real reasons! People with diabetes have been unhappy inside for many years before their diagnoses.

Many people ask me my definition of health. My answer is, "When a person cannot feel happiness in life, then this person is no longer healthy." If we have not felt happiness for a while, then whether or not we have been diagnosed with diabetes, we are sick. Again, I emphasize the holistic concept of health integrating body, mind, and spirit. If a person has a healthy body but lives a miserable life, then he is not truly healthy.

"You create your own reality" is the highest guiding principle of Seth's teachings. Everyone has the power to create their own reality, and our bodies possess strong self-healing abilities. From this regard, diabetes of course can be cured. Doctors are supposed to help patients activate their own self-healing abilities, rather than developing new drugs. The real cure comes from the transformation of our minds, where positive energy can improve our blood circulation and our metabolism and enhance our immune systems. Whether it is a chronic disease or cancer, we can gain true health if we transform our minds, break away from our own rigidity, understand the power of reality creation, and live joyfully.

Unhappiness Occurs When We Put Limits on Ourselves

Some argue that they know they should be happy, yet they don't know how. Even when they ask this question, however, I can see from their facial expressions that their hearts have already begun to soften. When we begin to learn and to grow, our hearts transform without our notice. When you begin to ask, "How can I be happy?" you are already on the path to happiness.

Many unhappy people are unaware that they are not happy. Maybe they only wonder why they have so many worries, why there are so many pains and so much stress in life. However, they do not realize that they are already in an unhappy life pattern. All unhappiness arises from self-limitation and rigidity. For example, we might have a rigid attachment to our identity, social status, fame, age, sex, etc. Many people, seeing how I look, wonder, "You look like a cheeky young shaver. Are you really a medical doctor? Have you really been promoting the Seth materials worldwide?"

This is happiness, and I am practicing what I preach. I have never been confined by my identity, age, or social status. Regardless of whether I were the president of a country or a grandfather of old age, I will continue to be frank and open, always speaking my mind. Age is a rigid concept, whereas our souls have no age. An eighty-something-year-old person who caught a cold might need to stay in the hospital for a month to recover. An eight-year-old child might be admitted into the hospital for pneumonia, yet he will be jumping up and down in three days. This is because the eight-year-old has no rigid age concept. He is naturally connected with the universe's energy and naturally believes that he is healthy. He places no limitations on himself.

An eighty-year-old believes in many rules and limitations. "Will I be bothering my son and daughter-in-law if I do this and that? How will young people think of me, an eighty-year-old, if I travel with them?" To be connected with our souls, we first must let go of the concept of age. We can be eighty years old with a twenty-year-old's mind and vitality. Whether you are housewives or office workers, you will eventually realize this: Illness and unhappiness are something we must face on our own.

Worries and concerns combined with practical life's pain and stress make us unhappy. After retirement, try to do anything that makes you happy: Maybe you could take a part-time job at a flower shop or at the local aquarium. Try more new activities, and life will change naturally! As long as what you do is not heinous, I often say, you can do anything. However, we tend to like to ask for trouble by always thinking negatively. At times, the older we get, the more rigid we become. For example, let's say we took an older person to a restaurant. In the next few days, we would hear him complaining about how the dishes were too salty, that the soup had no taste, and the chef was no good. Say we took an older person on a road trip. They would complain that the bed was too hard, the pillow was not soft enough, or the hotel was too noisy. These kinds of things repeat themselves and bring friction to the relationship between children and parents.

I believe that I am easygoing and that many people can see the "free spirit" in me. I am not confined by my identity or social status. I believe we eventually will be one with our inner selves. When we are imprisoned by pain and suffering, we should remember to return to who we are, to be who we are, and to be with what we truly feel. However, to be ourselves is not being selfish. When we finally return to who we are, we let go of lots of burdens, and our souls no longer conflict with our egos. The more we can express our soul's vitality, the more we can help others. Many people come to my clinic not to ask for a prescription but to feel my life's vitality. They wonder how I can live so happily and with such great creativity?

Be Free
There are two kinds of freedom. You can get the first kind of freedom through escaping. After you have es-

caped, you might think that you are free, yet you are imprisoned by even more pressure. The natural joy that comes from the bottom of your heart will give you the second kind of freedom. This kind of freedom allows you to do what your soul desires the most.

The universe has a clever design. When we finish a job that's been done to our heart's full content, even if we are completely exhausted, our souls are full of energy. This is why I think working is different from exercising, because we are in a different mood. Working can be laborious, such as mopping the floor, washing the dishes, cleaning the ceiling. On the other hand, we exercise because we want to and because we enjoy sweating.

Nevertheless, there are two reasons for exercising. You might think that you are exercising for your health's sake, yet deep inside, you know that you exercise because you are afraid of being ill. The first reason is pessimistic. For example, Americans love exercise, yet they also see many doctors. Many people exercise with the fear that if they don't, they will be ill. Because of such a belief, they are more prone to sickness if they don't exercise. On the other hand, many people exercise because they enjoy it. They can be in the mountains, see the clouds, encounter insects. Of course, this person is healthy because all of his body cells are exercising with joy. We should believe that exercise can improve our health, but even without exercise, we are

naturally healthy, too. Organic foods can provide healthy nutrition, yet as long as we have balanced meals, we are still healthy. As long as we are at ease with ourselves, neither exercise nor food will be issues.

Many people relate diabetes to high blood pressure or genetics. However, based on Seth's teachings, our minds can influence our physical bodies. When we can change our genetics <u>through changing our minds</u>, we can definitely cure chronic diseases. When we are happy, truly free, and open-minded, our blood sugar levels and blood pressure will regain their natural balance, and no drugs will be needed.

We all should have the freedom that truly comes from our inner voice. This kind of freedom allows us to do what we do, not because of responsibility, but because it is something that we want to do. If you want to be a responsible mother, then it is not because you have no choice. Instead, it is because you really want to be a responsible mother. Freedom cannot be gained through escaping. Freedom means that we can truly do what our inner selves want.

Release Your Soul's Vitality, Be Happy and Carefree

What is happiness? At each moment, can we listen to our inner voices? Can we release our worries and fear? Ask yourselves, "Are things really as serious as they appear?" Seth's teaching emphasizes "being in the state of

grace." We should feel that we live in the universe's grace everyday. Please encourage your friends to pursue what they love. As long as we have learned how to listen to our inner voices, life will lead us to the best possible path.

I have always kept a full schedule, and yet I am always full of energy. Many people wonder, "Are you not tired?" Outside of my clinic hours, I travel around, including internationally, to promote Seth's teachings. When I finish a talk, I am usually sweaty. Of course, I am tired physically, yet I am happy. What I do allows me to use my energy to do what my soul wants to do the most. This is happiness.

Use your energy, even if it means rolling in the mud like a little piglet. Why not? Every day is a new beginning. Everyone is free. You might be a parent, a daughter, a friend, or even the third party of a marital affair, but fundamentally we are free and joyful souls.

When we can be ourselves and express our soul's happiness, we can get rid of the shadows of diabetes. Many diabetic patients still have a lot of time ahead of them. Maybe it takes five years, 10 years, or even 20 years before you can truly live the life you want. Do not waste your time in long-term depression, which would turn what could be an interesting life into chronic suicide. Once we find our joy in life, we don't have time to waste on being ill!

with Dr. Hsu

Question: In addition to maintaining a happy mind, are there any other things we can do in our daily routine that can help us to be healthier?

Response: The highest principles are: eat several smaller meals through the day, and follow Seth's suggested sleep schedule.

1. Smaller meals (do not be too full nor too hungry for too long at a time): Eating too much at one time is not good for our digestive systems. Similarly, being hungry for too long is harmful to our bodies and will cause digestive issues. I suggest that you eat enough to get 60 to 70 percent full at each meal and that you eat four to five meals a day. You can adjust this according to your own situation.

2. Adjusted sleep schedule (do not sleep nor be awake for too long at a time): Sleeping for too long will leave people with foggy thinking and stiff joints. Similarly, to be awake for too long at a time will cause the accumulation of toxins that our bodies usually release during short rests. These toxins will cause quick tempers and an imbalance between the body and the mind. In addition to the main sleep during the night,

take one or two naps in the afternoon or evening. This is extremely beneficial to your health, and it is an important habit to have whether you are ill or not. An adjusted sleep schedule can help improve the mind and body balance, improve your concentration, and correct emotional imbalances.

➤ Reminder from Dr. Hsu

Ask yourself calmly, "In the past few years, have I felt a lot of helplessness and powerlessness in my life? At work, in my family, or in my important relationships, do I frequently repress my feelings? Have I had to compromise or give in a lot? Is this really a job that I like doing? Or am I simply doing it for practical reasons? Am I truly living the life that I want?"

Be in a calm mood first. No matter what the external reality might be, no matter what all the rules you have been taught all your life, no matter what your neighbors, family members, or friends might be telling you, ask yourself, "What is the truest voice inside me? What is the most real feeling inside?"

You must do this exercise. Only when you can hear your inner voice, only when you can be with your inner feelings, can you start living the life you want. Take one step at a time until you are fully recovered from diabetes.

Chapter 5
Liver Cancer, Liver Cirrhosis: Refuse to be a Gloomy Tough Guy

The root causes of liver diseases are not to be found in the organ itself. The root causes are to be found in the blockage of emotions and feelings. Love and hate are deeply entangled with each other, with no way out. Disease of the liver depicts a person who would rather confine himself with reason than let feelings run their course. This is one of the reasons why liver diseases are less common in women. Women are more comfortable with emotions: They are less afraid to show them; when they feel like crying, they cry. Women possess far more tools to express themselves emotionally than men do.

Liver diseases are among the top ten leading causes of death in Taiwan. Many body organs are on this top-ten list. Western medicines have a variety of treatments for these diseases. For example, people with heart issues might need bypass surgery. Kidney failure might require peritoneal dialysis or hemodialysis to help remove toxins in the blood. When our livers, burdened with complex functions, are in trouble, nevertheless, there is no dialysis machine that can help it. Treating liver diseases remains a bottleneck for Western medicine.

The Liver is the Biggest Chemical Factory in the Body

The liver is located inside the lower right ribs. The liver itself is full of blood vessels, and it is provided valuable protection by the surrounding ribs, for there is a high death rate in the case of a liver rupture. The liver is the biggest chemical factory in our body. It manufactures many nutrients and is the busiest organ in the body. The liver makes albumin, cholesterols, and fats among other things. The liver is also the only organ that can regenerate itself. If we cut out a part of our liver, it will regenerate over time. Liver transplants are becoming more and more common.

Many people think that bile is produced by the gallbladder. This is not true. The liver is the real manufacturer of bile. The gallbladder's job is to store, to concentrate and to secrete bile. When our red blood cells reach the age of 120 days and pass through the liver, the liver cells will break down these old red blood cells and release hemoglobins that are contained inside them. The hemoglobins are then converted into bile pigments and become bile. When bile ducts are infected and obstructed, this process is disturbed and will result in jaundice.

The liver has the capacity to detoxify. Waste products and toxins, including most drugs we take, are dismantled and processed by the liver cells. In case of failure of the liver's metabolism, we might fall into a hepatic coma.

Most of us have heard the term "fatty liver" before. This term refers to a condition that has become quite common in the developed world, one which we fear. I want to emphasize this: fatty liver is not a disease; it is a state of overnutrition.

All the nutrients that are absorbed into our blood stream by our digestive system will enter the liver and be disassembled and processed by the liver cells. The liver is like the main processing plant of nutrients. For example, food at the McDonalds in the USA will definitely taste differently than the food at the ones in Taiwan. In the food industry products that are exported to foreign countries all undergo changes to fit the local palates. Following this example, food that enters our bodies all get disassembled and reassembled in the liver, to transform the nutrients into useful substances for the body. These are metabolic processes called catabolism and anabolism. As we gain weight, the liver will begin to store fatty cells and become a fatty liver. These excessive nutrients will go to our thighs and abdomen, causing local obesity. A fatty liver is caused by excessive nutrients. We can control it by changing our diet and exercising. When we increase our exercise level and reduce our weight, the liver will automatically begin to use its stored nutrients.

The Liver is the Most Emotional Organ

It is well known that many Chinese people have hepatitis. In the past, blood screening techniques were not as well developed, and many people contracted hepatitis through blood transfusions. Hepatitis A and E are contagious and usually spread through contact with bodily fluids and infected food. Hepatitis B, C, and D are caused by inflammation of the liver and can be spread through blood and vertical infection, such as a mother giving it directly to her baby. Many people have had hepatitis. Without knowing that they had had hepatitis, some people recovered and developed antibodies. Others, however, become asymptomatic carriers.

In theory, hepatitis is an inflammation of the liver. However, what makes people the most fearful is what is called fulminant hepatitis. Fulminant hepatitis is not directly caused by the virus itself. Instead, it is the result of the rampant response of the immune system. Upon detecting the viral presence inside the liver cells, the immune system then sets out to destroy the viruses, but in the end it destroys the liver cells, too.

Many people ask why our immune system would function like this? One reason is because nowadays, people like to take a lot of medications. Taking an excessive amount of drugs can confuse our immune system.

However, from the holistic approach, our thoughts and emotions can affect how our bodies function. For example, when we are nervous, our hands sweat. Our emotions and our organ functions are connected. Often, organ failures are due to unprocessed emotions. The liver is the most emotional organ in the human body. When a person cannot freely express his emotions, this will affect his liver functions.

A seventy-two-year-old man came to see me. He was diagnosed with a 1.9 centimeter tumor in his liver. During our conversation, he mentioned that his oldest son has had epilepsy since he was nineteen years old. The son later immigrated to the U.S. and married. However, five years ago, his wife had an affair, and they divorced. The son returned to Taiwan and was looking to get married again; however, he has set his sight on non-Taiwanese women only.

I have seen many liver cancer patients in their sixties and seventies. They all have a similar wish, which is that their children can achieve success and win recognition. Minimally, they wish their children to make a decent living. Nevertheless, most of them are hurt when their children do not meet their expectations.

I told this old man, "The main reason for your liver cancer is related to the fact that you cannot let go of your worries and concerns for your son." He had devoted his entire life to taking care of a child with epilepsy, even sending him overseas. However, the child not only is divorced but also is living with someone of whom he disapproves. This is such a heavy blow, and he is very hurt. He is afraid to express his disapproval, fearing this will cause conflicts with his son. The son also respects and is afraid of his father. He has kept his distance from his father. They both love each other, yet they do not know how to be with one another.

Parents, with deep love and high expectations, wish that their children will have a bright future. When their expectations are shattered, the anger and hurt can do great damage to their bodies. Those who are not good at verbally expressing love are the ones with the deepest hurt. These people's core beliefs are: If my child is not well off, then it means nothing, even if I am successful. Shattered expectations turn into despair, anger and eventually depression. This is when the liver becomes ill. "You would rather die than watch your child's life go downhill," I pointed out bluntly. This is what is in his subconscious. The truth might be hurtful, but it is the truth.

If a person gets liver cancer or fulminant hepatitis while in his forties, fifties or older, then it is usually related to emotional pressure within the family. Our loved ones, who care the most about us, are also the ones who can give us the most pressure. Similarly, we might become angry at ourselves when we cannot meet their expectations. In the Chinese society, where family relationships are highly valued, many parents regard their children's success as their own glory. Many children grew up being constantly compared with their peers. This constant comparison could have damaged their self-confidence. Even when they become adults, they still cannot find their own values. They try hard to get their parents' approval. I have seen countless people like this. For example, one might take over the family business without knowing whether he truly likes this job. Or he might be doing this simply to gain his parents' approval. His life is hanging in the balance.

If a young person gets a liver disease, then it is mostly because he puts too much pressure on himself. Maybe he tries to fulfill his parents' expectations, while others might work day and night, only to strive for vindication. I know a family with eight liver cancer patients, of whom seven have passed away. Their father was not their grandfather's biological son, so their entire family had been looked down upon. When the father and mother both passed away, all the children were almost sent to the orphanage by the family elders. My client, one of the children, was determined to become successful, to have a better life than the rest of the relatives. He focused his life on earning more money.

Many people who endured hardship during childhood might end up doing a job that they don't like. They pursue fame and fortune for the purpose of winning over someone. They wish to feel pride and elation. But they never really feel the joy of success. They are lost in life and can only value what their society wants. When we work day in and day out for other people, then the burnout exhaustion will cause liver problems. But more deeply, we are angry at ourselves for failing to meet our own expectations.

"I cannot forgive myself; I should have done a better job; I cannot get vindication for my parents…." These angry emotions can turn into deep self-blame and desperation, which then turns into an attack on the liver. For example, many people tend to report only what is good, while concealing what is unpleasant. We might not want our parents to worry, and we might be afraid that we will lose face. Even when we feel we are wronged, are getting a divorce, aren't doing well, etc, we are unwilling to let our loved ones know. When we are disappointed in ourselves, depression starts to accumulate, and it is just a matter of time before the liver becomes sick.

I must emphasize this to everyone who is learning the holistic approach to health: We are the masters of the viruses. In the universe, there is absolutely no single virus that would make a person sick without reason. Those who are infected by viruses are not so because they are unlucky but because they already have a wound in their hearts.

Therefore, no virus wants to kill out of ill will nor without reason. For example, Hepatitis B does not want to afflict a person's liver with cirrhosis or cancer. When the person dies, so do the viruses. The viruses are not the problem. Even with vaccines, we cannot really prevent liver diseases.

Develop Your Inner Male (Animus; Yang) and Inner Female (Anima; Yin) Energies

A retired soldier came to see me a few years ago. He was in great pain because his wife had left him. He loved his wife very much, but he was trapped in his own male image. He was unwilling to put aside his own pride in order to win her back. He had so many unexpressed feelings buried inside, because he believed that a man should be macho. He passed away due to cirrhosis of the liver.

I think men who cry will reduce their chances of getting liver diseases by half. Most males are taught that men do not easily shed tears and that they should not reveal their vulnerability no matter what. It is such a paradox that many males feel they should maintain their macho image and should not express their love for people, as if showing emotion were a sign of weakness. As a result, many fathers, who love their children deeply, tend to scold their children for their wrongdoings, damaging their children's self-confidence in the process. The fathers then suffer from alienating their own children.

Males tend to be fixated on gender, self-image, and social achievement. Even at home, many men still wear the mask of the "boss." Not many males can hold their children's hands and say, "I love you so much! I love you no matter what!" They are unable to let their children know that they have fallen in love with them from the moment they were born. I often tell men that if you don't know how to cry, don't know how to express your emotions, then you are not a real man! Regardless of your gender, every person has both male and female characteristics. It is just a matter of how much each side is expressed.

Everyone has both male (animus) and female (anima) energies, as souls are both male and female. We must develop our inner male and female energies, allowing the energy to balance and integrate between our souls and our bodies. Before puberty, male and female characteristics are not as obvious and distinct. After puberty, the distinctions become clear. Menopause is the period when our inner Yin and Yang reharmonize.

As a female, we mainly learn to develop our Yin energy. However, Yin and Yang are one from the soul's perspective. For example, as a woman gets older, her voice might become deeper, her skin will change, and she might start to show more and more male characteristics, such as being resolute and steadfast. Similarly, as a man gets older, his facial profile might become softer, and he might become more even-tempered.

Liver diseases and cirrhosis of the liver reveal an unharmonized inner self. Some possible reasons are:

1. The inability to adapt to new role in life. A man may not be able to transition from a macho steadfast character into one with emotional expressions and feelings.

2. Blockage of love energy. This might be commonly seen in the Chinese family system. Children think they must be highly successful to make their parents proud. Many Chinese parents are disappointed in their children's achievements. Deep inside the parents blame themselves; however, outwardly they show repressed anger.

3. At the terminal stage of liver cirrhosis, fluid accumulates in the abdomen, which makes the patient look like a pregnant woman. Another symptom is called gynecomastia, an enlargement of the male breasts, due to a hormone imbalance which favors the female hormone. All these appear to be caused by the

liver. However, from the holistic perspective, they are caused by the unexpressed Yin or female energy. When this energy finds no outlet to express itself, it has no choice but to express itself through our bodies. When energy cannot be integrated in our conscious mind, cannot be expressed in our life, such an energy will not simply disappear but will be shown through our body's diseases.

As males grow into old age, if their feminine characteristics are not expressed, if they continue to be stiff, steadfast, and fixated on external status and their self-image, then their liver will also become stiff, and they will get liver cirrhosis. In order to cure liver issues, we must first be willing to go outside our "boxes," to return to the essence of our existence, and to be in touch with our true inner feelings. If we are able to allow our inner feelings to start moving again instead of being a stiff old man, then our livers will no longer need to become stiff, resulting in cirrhosis.

Children Are Not Supposed to be Obedient
Children are not supposed to be obedient, whether the instruction is from parents, teachers, principals, or experts. Children do not have to listen to any of these, because they must learn to listen to their own voice. Upon hearing this, many parents might flip out. But

you will discover how valuable this concept is in the future. Children can be disobedient, but this does not mean that they can commit a heinous crime, for example. Instead, this concept means that pieces of advice offered by parents and teachers are just suggestions. Children do not have to follow them. In the end, children must come up with their own decisions.

"Never Let Me Go" is a 2010 British film depicting a group of human clones intentionally created for the only purpose of becoming organ donors. Once their bodies have matured, they will be used as organ donors and die. Their entire life has been planned without any exceptions. They do not need to plan for the future, worry about what to eat or what to wear. They are raised as livestock, with no room to rebel. I am impressed with a scene in which several teenagers are trying to order a meal. This is their first experience out. While in the restaurant, they are at a loss as to how to order food. In the end, they all order the exact same drink and meal.

This particular plot impacted me tremendously. These clones appear to look exactly like normal human beings. However, they have fixed thought patterns. This reminded me of our education system in which there are too many fixed rules. Society's stereotype determines what to do and how to do things. Our children have been raised as "caged chickens." Yet, we expect that they will become an independent, self-responsible "free-range chicken" one day. Isn't this paradoxical?

Take me, for example. I seldom listen to my parents, even though I respect them. I listen to what they have to say, but I do not always follow their advice. I will take their opinions into consideration when I make my own decision. This is similar to how the liver disassembles nutrients coming from the digestive system and reassembles them into what the body can use. We can learn about how life works by observing how our body works.

Let's say that parents give their children suggestions. Children take everything "as is" without going through the "digestive" system where it is broken down and then absorbed. When children skip the step of coming up with their own opinions, problems are sure to arise further down the road. When one day they realize that they are doing a job that they do not like or are married to someone whom they do not love, resentment will grow. Such a negative energy will eventually cause the body to send out warning signs.

As an educator teaching the Seth material and the holistic concepts, I demand that my students do not have their own opinions in their first three years of study. They are in a period to digest, absorb, and integrate the content. They have not yet learned enough to argue with me. After three years, if students still do not have their own thoughts, then they cannot be my students. My students should integrate what they have learned in the first three years and come up with their own understandings. Similarly, each child should digest suggestions given by their parents and teachers and integrate them into their own ideas. Children will be healthy this way.

There is a Chinese saying, "There are no weak troops under a strong general." However, to apply this concept in family relationships would require a new interpretation. Usually when parents are overpowering, children are weak and lack confidence. Through the dominating parents' eyes, the kid can never do anything right. From the kid's perspective, he simply gives his responsibility over to his parents, as his parents will always take care of everything and make all the decisions for him. As a result, strong generals have only weak troops!

Parents who are overly responsible for their children's lives and who tend to make every decision for their children will be destined to have a life of toil. By doing so, they will also lose sight of their own lives, because they refuse to live for themselves. Everyone's journey on earth is one with its own adventure. When parents can let go of their children's lives, then they can finally begin their own journey.

Seth mentions that many children once believed that their parents are almighty. This belief is a convenient way for children to feel safe. Once they reach puberty, they realize that their parents are human and can also make mistakes. At that point, they are liberated from the belief that adults are always right and will not make mistakes. This means they will begin to face and overcome their own challenges.

Before puberty, children live under the protection of their parents. They follow their parents' ideas on what to eat and what to wear, and they usually accept them naturally. As they grow up, slowly they begin to walk their own paths. This is a very normal transition. Parents should learn to respect their children's decisions and should feel comforted that they are beginning to take their lives into their own hands.

Live a Life with Soul

Many people complain that I never directly provide an answer to their questions. This is because problems are here not for us to solve but for us to learn from. The Bible says, "Blessed are the pure in heart: for they shall see God." Everyone has the pure heart of a child, which will lead us to happiness. Follow your joyful impulses, feel free to be who you truly are. Begin to look at the world from different perspectives. When our hearts turn young, we will become energetic. This is the holistic approach to health that I have been promoting.

Do not treat your body like a machine which might need a liver transplant or a knee replacement, in the same way that we change a new tire or add lubrication to a car. Our soul sees each day as a joyful source of creation. Count your smallest blessings. Life can only be meaningful when we live each day to its fullest.

 **with Dr. Hsu**

Question: From the holistic perspective, do we still need to take vaccines?

Response: Under the current Western medical system, taking vaccines is useful. Nevertheless, holistically speaking, vaccines are not that useful. I often lecture, "Cancer is here to embarrass the Western medical system." No matter how medicine continues to develop, it still cannot cure cancer. Cancer forces the Western medical system to look at a disease beyond pure biology and to examine it from the mind, body, and spirit angle. The current Western medical system will not be able to cure cancer unless it takes the holistic perspective. The holistic approach believes that, like two sides of a coin, thoughts and emotions are the other side of cells. Our health requires both healthy life perspectives and healthy organs. Only examining a person's cells, organs, and performing scans is not the way.

These examinations and their data are only superficial and cannot see the depression, conflicts and sufferings in one's life. The Western medical system must awaken and recognize the fact that body, mind, and spirit are one. This is the only way to cure the diseases for which Western medicine cannot even find the causes. A vaccine is a form of a specific virus. Suppose I can give a patient a dose of liver vaccine to prevent liver diseases. However, can I prevent him from accumulating depressed thoughts? Furthermore, from the immune system's perspective, the more vaccines we inject, the more confused our immune system becomes. Nevertheless, based on Seth's teaching that "You create your own reality," if someone believes that vaccines work, then he can get some benefit from that vaccine. After I began to study Seth, I no longer took any vaccines. I have found a way that is more effective than the vaccine alone—we can give ourselves the belief that the vaccine is full of hope.

Question: What challenges would myoma of the uterus represent?

Response: Hysteromyoma is a benign growth of smooth muscle in the wall of the uterus. Symptoms will depend on the size and location of the growth. In the past, women were encouraged to bear children, and there were not many methods of birth control. Before menopause, a woman could experience childbirth many times. Many women spent half of their lives producing children. The uterus is a strongly creative organ. However, modern women, typically with one to three children, are not as "productive" as before. This organ no longer nurtures so many lives, yet its creative ability still exists. But what can it create? From the holistic view, hysteromyomas represent (1.) modern women's intention to break away from gender stereotypes and (2.) their longing for creative self-fulfillment. In today's modern society, women can create their careers as successfully as men do. Nevertheless, many women are still trapped by their gender.

Beliefs, such as "Women tend to be useless," "If you do try to build a career that fails, you will bring embarrassment into the family," "You are better off being a housewife," not only nag females but also become the barriers to self-fulfillment. Myomas grow on the most creative organ—the uterus—when a female cannot "create" otherwise. When the uterus stops bearing children and starts growing myomas, then this means that the woman is unhappy about her current situation. She is eager to create, yet she is unable to overcome her rigid beliefs. She feels helpless and powerless. Her energy is blocked. Myomas are here to tell women that their strong life force is not finding a way to express itself. Whether it is a new-born baby, a new career, or a new future, it all means the same from the holistic perspective.

Neither injections, oral medications nor surgery will cure the root issue of myomas. All diseases represent a current unsatisfied state of being. If you find your new balance point, break out of the box, and rediscover your joy in life, then diseases can be cured.

Then the next questions are, "Which box do you want to break out of? Do you have things you have always wanted to do but have encountered barriers? Are you eager to prove your own ability, yet have been afraid to try? Do you feel that you are being overprotected (or controlled) by your husband? Do you often think of yourself as useless or unaccomplished?" You must take action in order to redirect your energy. As such, diseases will be cured naturally.

I have studied the holistic approach for over 20 years and am particularly passionate about bringing awareness to the limited effects of western medical practices. I know the only way to cure a disease is to find the emotional conflicts behind it and to resolve related key issues.

➤ Reminder from Dr. Hsu

Remember that you must allow your deep feelings and emotions to be expressed. Stop being a tough guy. Furthermore, ask yourself if you feel insecure, if you fear that you are not good enough, or if you are worried that you will be looked down upon. Do you feel that you must work hard in order to get approval and love?

Fully express the inner self that is so passionate! No longer be afraid to show love or to express your longing for love, affection, and approval. No longer believe that by doing these things you are showing weakness. Refuse to be a gloomy macho man. Learn that admitting one's vulnerability is one of the bravest things one can do.

Chapter 6
Accidents: There Are No Accidents, Only Choices

Based on the teachings of Seth's material, no one is a victim of accidents. Instead, accidents reflect the reality we create for ourselves, which means we choose to live either in disaster or in peace. True prevention of disasters, either the natural or the human kind, should be sought in the spiritual dimension. Allowing for spiritual growth is the only way to absolute inner peace.

I once had a car accident when I worked as an intern in Taipei Veterans General Hospital. I got hit on the highway by a car from the opposite lane. I stepped out to check if there were any damages. Just when I was about to take some pictures as evidence, the other party took advantage of the fact that there were no witnesses around and came at me aggressively, even trying to snatch my camera away from me. Luckily, a police patrol car came by at that moment, so I immediately asked the policeman for help. By the time the policeman brought us all back to the station for statements, an older man showed up and said to me, "If you insist on pressing charges against my nephew, you'd better watch your back from now on." Upon hearing such an outrageous remark, I immediately demanded that the policeman take notes to be included in the official record, as I intended to add charges for intimidation.

Then the men were nervous and tried to explain. The offenders were two young men. Not only were they drunk, but one of them was also on probation. If I were to press charges for robbery, he would have to go back to jail. As a firm believer in "forgive and forget," apart from demanding monetary compensation to fix my car and my glasses which had been damaged in the attack, I decided to settle for a sincere apology and a symbolic penalty of one dollar. That's it—case settled!

An Accident Only Takes Place When All Essential Elements are Fully Matured

Most people might think that this was nothing more than an ordinary car accident. I know it was not. Right before the accident I was having an argument with my friend in the car. I was very upset and didn't know how to deal with it.

An accident only takes place when all the essential elements are fully matured! The beans only sprout when there is enough sun, air, and water. Your heart sets the "scenes" of every single incident of your life. Whether you are a happy camper or down in the dumps, your heart is the key to all events.

Looking back at the car accident, it was no "accident" at all. I was furious with my friend, so I had my anger released by being knocked down and beaten. That's why deep down I didn't blame them at all. They were just responding to my intention to develop the elements for creating the necessary scene. That, of course, doesn't mean that you are allowed to cause a car crash on purpose or beat someone up to make yourself feel better. The point is that we should understand how our psychic atmosphere could cause incidents.

For those who have experienced a car accident, try to recall your mental state prior to the "accident." In most cases, you were not quite yourself. Maybe you were unhappy because you had just had a fight with someone a few days earlier. Perhaps, you were frustrated because you were exhausted from working overnight and being underpaid. More or less, you can usually sense that a storm is coming way before something actually goes wrong. Your worries or paranoia are the crucial elements that make the "accident" mature.

Now let me give you another example. A few years ago my mother broke her clavicle, the collarbone, due to an accident. Yet right before the "accident," she found herself stuck in a dilemma. My mother needs financial security. She wants to stand on her own feet instead of relying on her children. However, as a mother, she felt obligated to help her daughter after her grandchildren were born. So she agreed to let her daughter pay her to babysit her grandchildren. She thought this would kill two birds with one stone.

Unfortunately, taking care of two energetic grandsons was really more than she could handle. In addition, she hardly had any free time, which meant no more time for karaoke or spending the day out with her friends. She wanted to quit her job, yet she was too embarrassed to admit it. She kept convincing herself that she was doing the right thing. She believed that she could not only show support for her daughter, but she could also make money on her own.

What a perfect time for an accident! She fell while riding her motorcycle and broke her clavicle. All problems solved! The incident gave her a way out. She didn't have to feel sorry about not wanting to help or about hurting their feelings. Everyone in the family told her to kick back and rest. My father even left work to take care of her. I myself also adjusted my schedule in order to spend more time with her.

This accident was not accidental at all! On the contrary, it came just in time! The "accident" gave her the perfect excuse to let go of the idea that she "should" go to work. As a result, she went with the flow and started to enjoy life. This is a perfect example of how you can untie the twisted knots tangled by your daily incidents and really live a life of wisdom.

Treat Your Family As a Collective Energy Field
Chinese people believe that a peaceful family will prosper. We didn't make this up out of nowhere. One has to treat his family as a collective energy field. A family may seem perfectly fine on the surface, but there can be devastating waves and currents running underneath. There can be emotional currents from miscommunication, and ignoring them may just collapse the whole energy field.

Many patients have come to my clinic for help because they wanted to heal the trauma after a sudden accidental death of a family member. There is always a story behind every family member's departure.

For example, many women don't have a life of their own until they get divorced. After the divorce, a woman gets to choose what kind of life she wants to live; she learns to become financially independent and to manage her own future. These simple facts reflect how a woman can suffocate within her marriage, when there is no room for her to stretch to her full potential.

On the other hand, the same rule applies to those widows who have lost their husbands in accidents. At least, it works the same way on the level of the subconscious. Some women live in the shell of protection with no chance to utilize their talents. Only the absence of her spouse will break that shell. Of course, the wife did not agree to lose her husband in her conscious mind. This agreement was made between both the husband and the wife at the spiritual level. After the husband's departure, the wife then can use her potential to take care of her family.

In Chinese folktales there are stories about those "meant to be widowed" women, whose husbands always die in an accident. Traditionally, people think that these women are cursed and that they bring bad luck and death to their spouses. Now let me tell you my version of the "meant to be widowed" story based on the holistic body-mind-soul principles. Once upon a time, there was a couple who were both bossy. Neither of them were willing to come second in their marriage. The husband wanted to take back the power and to be in charge, so he argued with his wife all the time. He wished that he could just divorce her; however, that was not an option. Subconsciously, he chose to die in an accident, leaving full control to his wife. As odd as it might seem, it is not a story of how a man was forced to die by a strong woman.

From the holistic perspective, it was a mutual decision! Every accident tells a family story. Let me give you some other examples.

There is a family with two children. The parents are not very rich and can barely support their kids. However, now the mother is pregnant again with their third child. This will definitely be a financial crisis for the whole family. Subconsciously, every family member chose to face this family issue as a challenge. In order to solve it, one of the family members may volunteer to "step down." That family member could be the third child still in utero, or it could be one of the two older children. To "step down" means to "leave" due to a sudden death caused by an accident. The death is not an accident at all, and I have seen similar stories among many of my patients.

Here is another true case. A little girl who was in first or second grade got hit by a drunk driver at her own doorstep. This accident fractured her lower leg bones. A few months later after the fractures were healed, the little girl started to become emotionally unstable. She ignored her family, refused to walk on the street, and was awakened by nightmares.

According to her mother, things got even worse after her daughter returned from the hospital. She used to cuddle and chitchat with her mother, but now she barely spoke to her.

Most doctors would diagnose this child with post-traumatic stress disorder. You now have a brand new perspective, which is "Everything happens according to the inner cause and effect." This broadens our investigation into the situation.

The first thought that came to my mind is that the little girl was angry with her mother! There are several possible reasons. First, the girl blamed her mother for not being with her when the accident happened. Second, she was not happy because her mother couldn't spend more time with her at the hospital. Third, before the accident, the financial situation of this family was not good. Her mother had had to go to work instead of staying home to take care of her. She concluded that her mother didn't care for her anymore.

Think of each of our inner worlds as a small individual universe and the physical world in which we live as the outer big universe. People are terrified by the facts that the outer big universe is unpredictable and that they can never know when they will be caught off-guard. However, for those who have begun to learn about the holistic principles through insight into their small individual universes, they learn to see the true cause and effect behind all accidents. Therefore, these people will feel safer and more peaceful inside.

Let's apply this thinking to the depth of the little girl's soul, right to the middle of her individual universe. At the time she started to feel insecure and unsafe, were there already signs of trouble at home? Did her sense of insecurity have anything to do with her parents' marriage? Did she hear her parents quarreling all day long, threatening to get a divorce? Those can be very frightening experiences for a small child. Or was it because her mother did not explain to her clearly why she had to go to work so often, leaving her to assume that her mother didn't want her anymore?

This doesn't mean that parents can never fight. But it is the responsibility of both parents to let their kids know that even if parents argue, it doesn't mean they will get a divorce. Even if they were to get a divorce, they should make it clear that they will never abandon their children. Parents should always communicate with their kids about the reality of the marital situation. It is critically important that the children know that they will never be abandoned.

Each and every one of us generates a force field around us. There are people who seem to attract trouble wherever they go, because the kind of force field that they generate is especially accident-prone. That's why they are always in some kind of trouble, such as getting involved in a car accident or a lawsuit.

Many people think it was just bad luck that the little girl got hit by a drunk driver. Yet the holistic principle already shows us how the cause leads to the effect. We are not talking about the common kind of cause and effect here, such as the principle of karma that exists in some religions. We are talking about the cause initiated in the mind and then manifested into an external event.

Most people assume the following: first a negative event happens; then unhappiness follows. However, such an assumption is wrong! If you'd assumed that the little girl was a happy camper who only turned unhappy after the car accident took her sense of security, you would be wrong! Going down this path of thinking only fuels the fear that security can be easily snatched away by a single event and prevents one from obtaining true ease and inner peace.

You have to start believing that there is no smoke without fire. Your heart is the fire, and what happens to you is the smoke. In this case, the little girl felt insecure first. She was afraid that her mother didn't want her anymore, and she was terrified of being abandoned. All of her beliefs triggered the car accident. Afterwards, the accident made her need her mother even more.

I told her mother that what was hidden behind this car accident was the silent plea of her child. Deep down in her heart, what she was trying to say to her mother was, "Please don't leave me, Mom. I am so scared! Would you please be here with me?" Children often have trouble expressing themselves verbally. So, this little girl transformed her silent plea into action, thus leading to the car accident. What she really wanted to say is, "I am afraid, Mom."

I suggested to her mother that she adjust her work schedule to coordinate with her child's needs. She should attempt to be there every day when her daughter comes home from school. She should sit down and talk to her daughter to make sure that she understands why she needs to go to work. The mother should let her know that she still loves her very much and that she will never abandon her. This was the only way to make her feel safe and secure. Otherwise, accidents will continue to plague this family.

Children Who Do Not Want to Grow Up
"I don't wanna, don't wanna grow up. There are no fairytales when I grow up. I don't wanna, don't wanna grow up. I would rather be silly and dumb…." This is in a song called "Don't Wanna Grow Up" by a popular girl band. The lyrics vividly descibe the sorrow that many of us carry within. When we were kids, all of us wished to grow up as fast as possible so that we could make our own decisions instead of being told what to do by our parents. However, when we are grownups, it seems that before we can really enjoy being free and independent, we become captives of responsibilities and expectations.

If given a choice, many of us would probably prefer to return to the carefree time of childhood. One of my patients managed to do just that through an accident! He was a young man who suffered permanent brain damage after a car accident. He became mentally disabled and exhibited silly and "crazy" behavior. The people in his community think he is a nut-case, and his family is deeply ashamed of him.

During one of our therapy sessions, I told him that I thought that he just didn't want to grow up. Suddenly, he became "normal" again and asked, "How did you know? I have never wanted to be the person whom my parents want me to be, one who takes full responsibility for the support of our family!"

As the only boy in the family, he had to deal with the expectations of his whole family. This was a heavy burden for him to carry. He had the secret desire to escape the obligations that come with being the sole heir, obligations that will only rise sky-high once he became an adult.

What a big secret to have! Is his car accident really just a simple "accident?" Every once in a while, we all wish to run away from real life, including myself. Postpartum depression, for example, could very well be a way to run away from the "motherly duty," or it might arise from feelings of fear or inadequacy, unsure of her ability to take care of a newly born child.

Everyone has a desire to be free, free from our responsibilities. We want to avoid life's pressures, bad relationships, or sometimes it is simply a desire to run away. Somewhere between wanting to run and not be-ing able to run is when accidents occur! Many people live their lives with blinders on their eyes. Only a minority of people have insight into the true essence of these incidents and realize the true cause and effect of accidents.

The young man in my case was not ready to take responsibility for his life. If he were again pressured to do so, a second accident would definitely occur!

The happiest time of his life was his childhood. Even though the accident meant that he could not be a normal man, this was a consequence with which he could live. Nothing would really improve unless he chose to change his mind.

Not every child wants to grow up to be an adult. For many patients with psychoses such as schizophrenia, bipolar disorder, and major depressive disorder, the first signs of their disease appear around their teen years. This is the transitional age of turning from childhood into adulthood. This is not a disease, but a manifestation of a child who does not wish to become a grown-up.

When a parent comes to me for these kinds of issues, I tell them that they must change the concept that their children must become a responsible adult.

You can expect your children to be able to take care of themselves. However, do not insist that they get married, have children, or accomplish social achievements. These people just want to enjoy life; they don't want too many obligations.

As a matter of fact, many of us want to remain a child and stay irresponsible. However, some of us learn well and are able to become responsible adults. Others don't manage as well in getting through this transitional process. For those who already have trouble making their way through this transformation, the more pressure that is put on them, the greater the chance that they will have mental disorders, accidents, or even suicides.

The souls of these children signed up for an earth adventure in order to enjoy life. They never wanted the harsh side of adult life, so they live using their own principles of cause and effect. When this principle involves someone else, we call it *Nidana*, which in Buddhism means a chain of causation. It's not a sad thing at all for a parent to have such a child. On the contrary, the parent may actually benefit from the child who has reminded them of the simple joys of life.

If you happen to be one of these parents, there is no need to suffer. Instead, experience the pure happiness of taking care of your child. Having already grown up, you know all the sorrows of being an adult. Let your child who refuses to grow up become the compensation, reminding you of how it feels to be innocent once again. This will help to free you from all of your daily duties and to bring pure happiness back into your life.

You can live a miserable life because you have a child who has a mental disorder or low intelligence, or you can see it as an opportunity to change your lifestyle and laugh out loud with your child instead.

Stop trying to force such a child to live an ordinary life, to find a job like everyone else does. It will only bring misery to everyone. If only you can see things in a different way and start to live out the joy of life, then the mental state of your child can improve, too. Your whole family will be happy again.

Often we become too reasonable and responsible, and we forget to feel our happiness inside. There is nothing wrong with being responsible, yet it is equally important to celebrate life by enjoying ourselves.

Death Can Be a Mercy

When a mother mouse bears too many baby mice, she will eat some of her babies to make sure that the others have a better chance to survive. She knows that she won't have enough milk for all of them, nor would there be enough space for all of them to grow. If she tries to keep them all, they may all end up dead. So it is not a cruelty at all, but it is a biological instinct and a mercy to prevent them from starving.

The human population on earth has already exceeded seven billion. We do not feel less alone because we have more people around us. Instead, we become more distanced from each other, because more people means more competition. There does not seem to be enough jobs or enough houses for everyone. Worst of all, there does not seem to be enough space for all of us. The earth seems to be worn out in her efforts to accommodate us all. Human beings have abused all of earth's natural resources and taken up all of the living space that rightly belongs to other animals and creatures on this planet.

According to some social studies, if the population continues to grow, it is only a matter of time before the human race dies out. Either we will engage in a global war which will wipe out most of us, or we will be eliminated by a series of natural disasters. I am sure we all remember the horrible tragedies such as the tsunami in Southeast Asia and the super-earthquake in Japan. Another potential way to cause many casualties is the severe infectious diseases which we see all around the world.

Seth once told us in his books that people in this world have lost themselves and think of themselves as victims of natural forces. Natural disasters or man-made tragedies are the mirror that reflects such bitterness inside the collective consciousness of all mankind. Our mental state has become worse and worse, as we believe that we have to struggle hard to live through another day.

What heartless tsunamis and earthquakes to take away human lives; what a cold-blooded God to allow vicious infectious diseases to proliferate in our world! We are wrong about that! This is a mutual agreement made between human beings and the universe! Everyone chooses to leave this earth for his own reasons.

When a large group of people chooses to leave earth, it is because a collective decision was made by all of humanity. Here is a similar analogy: You decide to go out for dinner, but the restaurant you have chosen is already filled with people. In addition, there is a long line waiting outside, so some of you may choose to leave because it's too crowded. It takes deeper wisdom to be able to read the cause and effect of a mass event than it does for a personal one.

Accidents Speak for Love

Why do natural disasters always happen on top of chaos? Because the universe says: "You people like to create wars in order to kill each other. Stop it and blame me! Blame me for whatever happens. Natural disasters will unite you and allow you to show your love through actions to help one another." So every time I watched the news reporting natural disasters or man-made tragedies, I saw no hazard but the chain of cause and effect beyond it. Seth says that, from the collective spiritual perspective, all human beings are one. As long as there is still one person suffering, then the rest of humanity cannot be truly happy.

When there is a disaster, help will flood into the area that needs it the most. You can see compassion and love coming in from all corners of the earth. Those places that have been long forgotten suddenly get all the help and resources because of this incident.

For example, suppose in Taiwan there was a huge gap between the rich and the poor. People who live in the middle of the island are extremely poor, yet the people who live in the north and south ends of the island are very rich. What will happen to this island next? There will be a huge earthquake or a fatal infectious disease in the center of the island, which creates an opportunity for the people of the north and the south to express their love and support to their fellows. This is what is going to happen in the future, so look closely and pay attention to your surroundings.

Since I first started my studies integrating holistic principles and the Seth material, I have wanted everyone to know that it is possible to perceive the dynamics of the world's future from your own insights. This will eliminate the feelings of powerlessness and being lost. Furthermore, we will start to see the true nature of life and to understand every cause and effect. We'll realize that if we don't stop sabotaging the earth and start to make changes now, there will be no future for any of us! The earth is to be shared by all life forms. It is not the exclusive property of human beings. The rebound of nature's force is not any kind of revenge at all, but it is there to show us greater love and patience.

Develop Your Sixth Sense

We all hope to live in peace, but often we live in fear, instead, and not without cause it seems. In recent years one natural disaster seems to follow the next. Understanding true cause and effect will help to alleviate fear. Remember the cardinal rule: Only when the conditions are met in the inner world, will accidents happen in the outer world. The people who fell victim to natural disasters were not victims at all. In the largest classroom of life called the earth, those people willingly chose their own curriculum, so to speak. In other words they chose their own way to leave earth. Some of you cannot help but ask, "Dr. Hsu, I don't think I had any inner conflicts at all, and yet accidents still happened to me!"

Here is my answer: In order to be aware of your inner beliefs, it takes time to practice. You have to progress step by step, day after day. It is a lifetime learning process.

Yet, I do have a few tips to help you along the way. There are two lifestyle principles that I advocate passionately, which I call knacks of keeping vitality:

"Don't overeat; don't starve too long." Allow a balanced diet intake in a 24-hour period.

"Don't stay awake too long, and don't sleep too long." Allow several short sleeping sessions during the day.

Vitality plays a role in being able to sense the workings of both the inner and the other (physical) world. Keeping vital will keep you from falling victim to random disasters. In respect to the topic of "Develop Your Sixth Sense," the latter is the most relevant. A short period of sleep keeps you more alert and develops the sixth sense that most people do not retain after childhood.

We are all familiar with the concept that animals can predict (natural) disasters. Humans also have the same potential ability. In order to use it reliably, we must start working with it. Several short sleeping sessions during the day help to develop this ability and slowly bring out our primal instincts. Someone who inserts several short sleep sessions into his overall sleep pattern will respond faster to imminent danger than other people. He senses danger before it happens. For example, you are driving on the highway when out of the blue you decide to switch lanes. The next thing you know, the car that had been ahead of you has an accident. That thought urging you to change lanes is your sixth sense. It is a feeling that you just can't explain.

This is an ability you can develop! Your brain is usually quite dull when an accident happens. After you start the habit of having short sleep sessions, your consciousness becomes more alert and your reactions more precise. Before an incident actually occurs, you will already have sensed the danger, and you will not feel overwhelmed by the incident the moment it occurs. You might even already have started to react in such a way that diverts the worst danger away from you.

In public education, all of the emphasis is on teaching the public how to avoid accidents and to avoid attracting infectious diseases. "Check, check, double check. Wash your hands frequently and thoroughly." The question is, does one really feel safer after repeatedly checking, for example, doors or repeatedly washing one's hands? One might see a parallel with obsessive compulsive disorder (OCD). Those who suffer from OCD constantly live in fear, causing them to check endlessly locks, doors, windows, bank accounts, etc. Some wash their hands compulsively because they are consumed by a fear of germs.

Life can't be great if you spend every second watching your back and constantly worrying about what might happen. It is a good thing to stay alert. However, life won't have any meaning if you are on high alert all the time and drive yourself crazy!

I urge you to go back to your core family, go back

to your inner world, and ask yourself the following questions. Do you feel peaceful inside? Is your inner universe a safe place? Have you accumulated lots of negative seeds inside that are ready to sprout into accidents?

The holistic view on cause and effect is totally different from the traditional religious one. The holistic principles focus on the cause, which originates from your heart, whereas the religious ones focus on the effect, which is often seen as a punishment for bad behavior.

Traditional religions use karma and punishment to describe cause and effect. Yet, from the holistic perspective, we don't categorize cause and effect into good and bad, because they are nothing but true reflections of each other.

According to the teachings of the Seth material, there are no accidents. You create your own reality by the rule of cause and effect. Therefore, you create your own disasters or your own happiness. So, start to grow your own spiritual seeds by learning the holistic principles. Let them grow into big trees to shade your spirit in peace. That is the ultimate solution to living in complete peace!

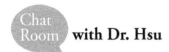 **with Dr. Hsu**

Question: What is your opinion and suggestions about the aging population?

Response: Our government tries to encourage child-bearing to balance the aging population. However, I have to say I disagree with this policy!

Older people are not a burden to our society. On the contrary, they are our treasury because they are fully mature holistic people. We should encourage them to contribute their wisdom and creativity instead of staying home and doing nothing.

It is already a dated concept that human beings breed their next generation to support themselves during their senior years. It's a difficult task for a young man to support himself nowadays, not to mention supporting his parents as well.

In this era of excessive population, one should decide to have a child because he wants to experience the joy of life and to welcome the arrival of a new soul. Birth encouragement can never solve the problems of an aging population. Instead, we must encourage the elders to live creative lives.

➤ Reminder from Dr. Hsu

Do you fill your heart with violent thoughts and emotions? Do you harbor lots of anger inside? If your answer is "Yes" to either question, sit down and calm yourself. Gently remind yourself not to pile up all these dangerous, high-density emotions. Alternatively, talk to someone, curse and cuss all you want, release frustrations by punching pillows, or do whatever you think is appropriate, as long as you don't repress your emotions since that will only lead to bad things happening to you.

Do you often think that you are a victim of misfortune, of ruthless mother nature, of original sin, or the violence and cruelty in human nature? Are you a pessimist who feels sad and/or cynical? Did you answer "Yes" to any of these questions? If so, be aware that disaster might be just around the corner! But don't worry. Once you are willing to change, you can re-create your own future!

Chapter 7
Pneumonia & Lung Cancer: Discover Your Sensitive Self

From the holistic body-mind-spirit perspective, lungs are organs that keep themselves moisturized by using the energy of love that is present in the air that flows through them. When we engage ourselves in never-ending battles as mistakenly perceived as necessary in the law of Survival of the Fittest, there is no room for love and affection. Problems particularly arise when the longing for love and approval from our parents is not fulfilled; in this instance our lungs tend to dry out to a dangerous level. This is when problems arise.

A patient of mine who was diagnosed with lung cancer once told me that when he was still a child, he would run out every day and wait for his father to come home. However, once he heard the sound of his father's motorcycle, he would rush back home immediately and pretend nothing had happened. He continued to do the same thing for many years, yet his father never knew his son eagerly awaited his return home every day. He loved his father so much, how he longed for affection from his parents!

So I asked him, "Why don't you tell your parents directly how much you need their love?" He answered, "What makes them happy is my making more money!

What they care about is my social status and bank account! I don't believe they can love me for real!"

His answer was heartbreaking to hear, yet his case is not an uncommon one in my experience. I have heard many stories of middle-aged lung cancer patients who outlive their parents. These people had a need that was never met, a need that all young children have: to feel the love from their parents.

Our Respiratory Systems and Its Intimate Relationship with Air

I often use the following metaphors: Air is "love," and earth is "life." The earth's surface is covered by air, which supports life. When there is no air, there is no life. We breathe air through our respiratory system; this is an extraordinary intimate relationship. Before we further discuss the link between body, mind and spirit, let me introduce some basic concepts about the respiratory system.

The respiratory system consists of airway tracts and a pair of lungs. The respiratory system is involved in the intake and exchange of oxygen and carbon dioxide between an organism and the environment. The upper respiratory tract consists of the nasal cavity and a group of four pairs of sinus cavities in different locations inside the skull. When the sinuses are inflamed and discharging inflammatory fluids, this condition is sinusitis; if the symptoms persist, it turns into chronic sinusitis. Chronic sinusitis is quite difficult to treat, as neither surgery nor medication is a sure cure.

The functions of the sinuses are:

1. to act as a resonance chamber for making sounds, just like the hollow space inside violins and cellos. Someone who suffers from sinusitis will sound nasally, because of the inflammatory fluids that obstruct the sinuses.

2. to reduce the weight of the skull. The sinuses are cavities filled with air, resulting in a reduction of the weight of the entire skull. The distribution of weight is thus better compatible with the erect posture of the human species.

3. to produce mucus and strengthen the immune system, by eliminating particles, bacteria and viruses.

Air enters the human body through the trachea and arrives at the pulmonary alveoli. If all alveoli present in one single person were to be spread out, the acquired surface would be equal to the size of a soccer field. Gas exchange takes place at the alveoli. Oxygen molecules pass through the membranes of the alveoli and attach themselves to hemoglobins, the iron-containing oxygen-transport proteins that reside within red blood cells. This is how oxygen transfers from the airway to the bloodstream.

By the way, the bond between hemoglobin and carbon monoxide is stronger than the bond between hemoglobin and oxygen. So when the air contains both carbon monoxide and oxygen, the hemoglobin will bond with carbon monoxide and fail to bond with oxygen, thus causing hypoxia. This is the reason for carbon monoxide poisoning, the treatment of which is to provide oxygen.

I highly encourage people to breathe through their noses. Among all the various parts of the human body, the respiratory system makes the most frequent contact with the outer world. The mucous membrane inside the nasal cavity produces mucus, which traps any particles that enter the nose through the air. The mucus can then be discharged. Another advantage of breathing through the nose is that the outside cold air warms up while passing through the nasal passages so that the cold does not directly impact the lungs.

The entire respiratory tract is lined with mucous membranes which produce mucus. This is a highly effective defense and healing mechanism of the human body! People often mistake "coughing" with "being sick." We need to change our way of thinking and tell ourselves: "My body is working hard towards healing itself!"

Coughing is a strategy of our body to get rid of unwanted substances. Coughing produces an increase in pressure in the lungs, pushing unwanted substances outwards. The same is true with fever; by raising the body temperature, it enhances the immune system and clears away waste products from the body. Coughing and fever are not signs of weakness of the body; but strategies for self-healing and releasing of negative energies.

The respiratory system is the first line of defense of the human body; it responds rapidly to changes in the environment that potentially affect the human body. In crowded, polluted cities when people wash up before bedtime, they will often find their towels turning black from all the dirt that clung to their faces and inside their noses.

Seth once spoke about how the mucous membrane inside our noses deliberately picks up small amounts of toxic material that are present in the environment. The purpose is to increase and enhance the immune system of the body. By breathing air through the nose, the nasal cavity continuously collects data so that the body can maintain an optimal balance with the outer environment. Many of us are city dwellers, and although we breath in polluted air every day, our bodies have adapted for the most part to this polluted environment.

The human body is simply ingenious. Behind the first line of defense mentioned above, there are enormous amounts of white blood cells that are present throughout the entire respiratory tract. So, our health is guarded by many lines of defense.

The Relationship between Cells and Thoughts
After studying the Seth material, I still catch a cold occasionally, once in one to two years. It is a sign I take seriously. I would consciously tell myself to have a good rest. Also, I would take the opportunity to review my schedule to make sure I hadn't pushed myself too hard and to make more time for leisure activities.

I certainly do not see having a cold as having an "illness" but as an adjustment that my body is making. It also serves as a reminder to evaluate carefully my stress level and the quality of my life.

Western medicine divides the respiratory system into two parts: the upper respiratory tract and the lower respiratory tract. Pneumonia and lung cancer occur in the lower part, while the common cold occurs in the upper one.

We all know that a cold will not kill you, but potential complications are not to be taken lightly. For those who are already showing early signs of a cold, it is beneficial to rinse your mouth with warm salty water twice a day. Gargling is particularly effective. These are good routines to have in one's overall personal hygiene.

The body often uses a cold to readjust its own

energy reserves. In the absence of severe complications, I would suggest taking the supportive approach: rest and replenish fluids and electrolytes.

Many people prefer to get an IV (intravenous fluids), because they find it comforting to watch the nutritious fluid enter their veins. On a psychological level this does have merits, but realistically it is no different than drinking a bag of fluids. In my opinion, a bottle of an isotonic sports drink works even better and is certainly safer!

Intravenous administration of fluids bypasses the digestive system and delivers the fluids directly into the bloodstream. Yet there is no guarantee that the fluids themselves have not been contaminated during the manufacturing process or that they have not expired. Intravenous administration is a forceful way for the body to absorb substances! Fluids that are orally administrated will first pass through the digestive system. When the body detects something wrong with the fluids, it will still have ways to expel them, either by inducing the gag reflex or by means of diarrhea.

As a matter of fact, nothing guarantees you perfect health, not even regular checkups, nutrient supplements, or exercise regimes. When you fall ill, reaching out to the medical profession for help alone will not work; you must reclaim your own power within. Based on the holistic principle, the power with which we create our diseases is the same one we use to cure it. We possess the power to create diseases, but we also possess the power to cure those same diseases. Even if you are perfectly healthy right now, you should hone your understanding of the holistic principles. You never know when you might need them. That is why I work so hard to study the Seth material and to promote the holistic principles.

I once read about an organization called "The Centenarians' Club of Longevity C." The members of this organization are all over one hundred years of age, among them are many who have always smoked and drunk alcohol.

I mention this not for the purpose of encouraging you to drink and smoke, but to point out that these external factors are not key components to health. Allow yourself to be happy and find the core value and purpose of your life. This is the sole secret to longevity. Those centenarians are without exception people who are full of smiles. The correlation between longevity and lifestyle is not absolute.

Establish this fundamental belief: Your thoughts are as important as your cells! In the holistic, body-mind-spirit view, thoughts equal cells. In other words when you think beneficial thoughts, you create healthy cells.

Good thoughts boost the morale and strengthen

the immune system. Nowadays, more and more people fall prey to diseases involving the immune system. This trend is caused by people accumulating too many insecure thoughts.   Take the current state of society: Some people think it is safe, while others think it is dangerous. It all depends on one's outlook. Clearly, our thoughts have a huge influence on us. You can provide your cells with the best living environment, such as clean air, a balanced diet, and daily exercises, but as long as you continue to think negative and pessimistic thoughts, your cells will never become completely healthy.

Whether or not our cells are healthy does not depend exclusively on the nutrients we take in. It's similar to raising a child. In addition to basic care, such as food, clothing, shelter and transportation, you still need to provide the child with love, encouragement, and acceptance. If you include all of these, you will have a mentally and physically healthy child.

This is why people still can get sick, despite having a good living environment, healthy diets and plenty of exercise. Without fully recognizing this fact, Western medicine will continue to get stuck in bottlenecks and experience a sense of powerlessness.

The Only Cure is Never Stop Learning the Holistic Way

In the past, pneumonia had been a major cause of death. People rarely die of pneumonia or pulmonary tuberculosis these days. However, we do see these words on the death certificates of our family elders: "cardiopulmonary failure" or "pneumonia induced sepsis."

At the terminal stage of certain diseases, many patients suffer from respiratory failure and require either tracheostomy or intubation. Tracheostomy is a surgical procedure in which a small incision is made in the trachea. Through this incision a tube is inserted which allows the patient to breathe either on his own or assisted by a ventilator. This also allows the phlegm that often obstructs the trachea to be sucked out. Those who need a tracheostomy may have a tumor high up in their respiratory tract, e.g. mouth or throat, which blocks the air from flowing in.

Intubation is the procedure in which a tube is inserted through the patient's natural airway, that is, through the mouth, the throat, the vocal cords to the depth of the trachea. However, any tube that is inserted into the human body can easily induce infections due to the germs and bacteria that inhabit the surface of the tube. The human body is programmed to get rid of anything that is foreign to the body. Often the tube that is widely used for IV itself is the source of infection.

Any infection of the lungs can lead to sepsis, which is commonly seen in patients relying on a ventilator. As a result, many times when lung diseases become fatal, it is not because of the disease itself but because of the process of the medical treatment.

The most frequently seen fatal lung disease is lung cancer, and adenocarcinoma is the most common form of lung cancer. Our respiratory tract is covered with epithelial cells that secrete mucus, also called gland cells. The term adenocarcinoma is derived from "adeno," meaning "pertaining to a gland," and carcinoma, which describes a cancer that has developed in the epithelial cells. Many cases of lung adenocarcinoma show that there is not an absolute association between lung cancer and smoking. (Smoking does have a strong association with a form of lung cancer that is called mesothelioma.)

Lung cancer, liver cancer and ovarian cancer are the types of cancer with no early warning signs. By the time you are diagnosed with one of these, usually you are already in an advanced stage of cancer. At the same time that the patients have to take in the news, they also have to face the possibility of death. The only suggestion your doctor can provide you is to enjoy the time you have left and to live out your life as happily as possible.

The treatment process of lung cancer is extremely tough. Especially in the final stage, cancer cells often metastasize to the brain, sometimes even leading to compression of the optic nerves. Western medicine is rendered helpless when treating patients in the final stage of lung cancer.

In hospitals, no doctor will tell you, "Your cells are very unhealthy, and, based on the results of the lab tests, we believe that your negative and pessimistic thoughts have caused your cells to mutate." However, this is the key to any treatment!

With so many years spent studying the Seth materials, I often wonder if there is a better treatment for cancer. After many years of observation and case studies, here is my take: To have a better chance at recovering from lung cancer, one must begin to embrace the holistic body-mind-spirit principles and to take steps on the journey of continuous learning and growth.

Nourish Your Lungs with Love

"From a young age I have always been the most responsible, the hardest working and the most giving member of my family. Why did my parents love my siblings the most, and not me?" Many of my lung cancer patients have said this very thing to me. Their chief disappointment and complaint is about their parents not loving them enough.

Therefore, as a reminder to all parents, treat all your children equally. Don't make the older children concede to their younger siblings, because you think the younger children "don't know any better." At the same time don't make the younger children obey their older siblings, because you think the older children "always know better." Let go of the stifling rules of "the older children always take care of the younger ones" and "the younger siblings must always pay respect to the older ones."

Even more important, don't treat your children differently according to their accomplishments. All of them should be loved without discrimination. Don't require the most "successful" one to take care of the other siblings financially. This only distorts the siblings' relationships with each other. Each child is unique in his own way, and parents should try to understand and to appreciate them from all angles.

Most of my lung cancer patients have similar backgrounds. They are in their mid-fifties to sixties, and they grew up in a fairly poor family with lesser living conditions. They live by the motto of "no work, no pay." They see life as a battlefield. A patient of mine even called himself a "fighting cock!" In the workplace, he had always fought his way up, trampling on others. It was the only way he knew to advance his career. He has always lived with the fear of being eliminated out on the battlefield that is called life.

From the holistic perspective, this reasoning has two sides. To remain competitive by working hard and striving to better oneself is a good thing. However, it turns into a bad thing when you live in constant fear of elimination from the competition if you don't work hard enough. This way of reasoning only leads to immense pressure on yourself. The true cause of lung cancer does not lie in the physical dimension. The true cause of lung cancer lies in the distortions that have occurred in one's thought system. This patient has created a very painful outlook on life for himself.

After understanding that the relationship between my "gamecock" patient and his parents was built on an "external standard of achievement" and a lack of love, I told him, "Go home and tell your parents that you are dying of lung cancer! Find out if they love you or not."

"I can't!" This man who was fearless in the workplace was cowering now. "I am afraid that, when they find out about my inability to work, they will love me even less."

Still, I continued to encourage him. Finally, he confessed his illness to his parents and expressed his feelings. Happily, he found out that his parents did love him! I believe this was the turning point in his recovery. The initial prognosis was that he had less than nine months to live; however, by now he has survived for more than five years! More importantly, he feels healthy and strong. He does not depend on gruesome chemotherapy to suppress his illness. By changing his way of thinking, he totally created a new life for himself.

"The Dream of the Red Chamber" is one of the greatest novels in Chinese literature. One of its classic protagonists is a woman named Lin Dai-Yu. Upon hearing the news of the marriage between her love Jia Bao-Yu and Xue Bao-Chai, she became so upset that she coughed up blood and died. Using modern medical knowledge, we now know that she died of pulmonary tuberculosis.

Lin Dai-Yu was an extraordinarily beautiful woman whose life ended tragically. She was a proud woman with a strong personality; however, deep down she suffered from low self-esteem. Combined with a melancholic nature and a low EQ (Emotional Quotient), she wasn't able to cope with the impossibility of marrying the love of her life. At the end she died despondently.

Love is a subject that has troubled mankind for thousands of years! We all want to love and be loved; but when we look at interpersonal relationships only as a source of brutal competition and mistrust, even the purest forms of love become tainted. Our perceptions become distorted. We start to believe that materialistic wealth is the highest attainable goal in life. We start to believe that wealth is the only reason for our parents to love us and for other people to respect us. When we are not satisfied with our accomplishments, we are bound to feel unhappy. The inner conflicts that rage within us can eventually lead to illness.

We all know how extremely important cows are to farmers in agriculture. An entire family's survival may depend on one single cow. Gratitude to these hardworking animals is the reason why many people do not eat beef. Farmers treat cows as a part of their family.

All living creatures need love. Animals need love. Human beings definitely need love. Chinese people often talk about "Chi." In a way it means the energy of love! If we want to care properly for our lungs, we need to work on our outlook on life in two major areas.

First, create meaningful relationships by communicating with authenticity and feelings. Many lung cancer patients believe that life is a matter of survival, that only work gives meaning to life. In some ways, they have a rather utilitarian outlook on life. These people tend to fail to find meaning in life when they enter retirement and often die soon after they retire.

My observation about them is that they spend a lot of time on work and worry. They don't know how to really live. All they do is worry about the rising crime rate or about the future of their children. How are they are going to survive in this competitive and dangerous world? They look at the future only with fear. They have no hope. They do not live; they survive.

I have often said that survival is the last thing you need to worry about. We all signed up for a journey to earth to learn and to enjoy life. You will always find a way to survive. It is the wisdom of living a life that needs to be learned.

Second, believe and trust that you are worthy of love. As mentioned earlier, lungs are organs that keep themselves moisturized by using the energy of love that is present in the air that flows through them. If we focus too much on being competitive for survival, we lose the nourishment of that emotional moisture. In particular, if our thirst for parental love is not met, our lungs will dry out and become ill.

We must change our thinking and start to believe that we are worthy of love. Get rid of the sense of inferiority. We are all unique individuals, and we are all worthy of existence.

Examine Your Emotional Conflicts

We already know that the respiratory system is connected to the energy of love. When a child suffers from a persistent cough with no apparent physical cause, I would advice the parents to try talking to their child. See if he is troubled inside with any emotional issues. See if there are things he wants to say but has never been able to express them.

As I have described in my previous book "Connections between Mind and Diseases," coughing is the result of suppressed emotions that are trapped inside the chest. It is like a barrel of resentment stuck inside the chest cavity.

I had a patient who had struggled with tinnitus for five to six years. He had been to doctors and taken medicines, yet the symptoms just kept coming back. I asked him if there had been any major event in his life before the onset of tinnitus. He was stunned by my question. After a while he recalled that six years ago his father had died of a heart attack.

"Do you blame yourself for that?" I asked.

I bet you already know the answer. This patient had been blaming himself for his father's death the past few years. He blamed himself for not having noticed his father's illness earlier. He believed that if he had gotten his father to the hospital sooner, he might have survived! He especially regretted not having made better use of the time he had with his father when he was still alive.

"This is why you have tinnitus! Your ears have

been buzzing with your voice of self-blame for the past six years!" My patient burst into tears the moment he heard me say this.

The voice of self-blame that had been bothering him turned into tinnitus. If he could start to face his guilt, the tinnitus would gradually diminish. I also made him understand that the sudden death of his father was not accidental. It was of his own choosing.

The ways people die often match their personalities and traits. Some people refuse to live a life that is spent lying in bed and depending on others even for the most basic needs. My patient's father chose to die suddenly from a heart attack. This was the way he chose to leave this life. We can mourn the deceased, but there is no need to blame ourselves for their deaths.

We tend to evaluate diseases through the limited scope of existing bodily symptoms; however, if we wish to better understand the root causes of diseases, we have to broaden that scope to include our mental world, thereby taking our inner thoughts into consideration.

Many symptoms do diminish during the course of medical treatment, but there might be other contributing factors in play than the treatment per se. For example, inner conflicts or dilemmas may have been resolved in the meantime, or feeling the support from doctors and family may have made way for love to flow freely again. Changes in frames of mind play an extremely important role in the recovery of one's health. Diseases can be cured without medical interventions.

I have often said that having regular health checkups done is okay, but you have to pay attention to your attitude towards doing them. Many may find it strange to hear this from someone like me, a trained family physician who used to do all kinds of checkups. Indeed, the early detection of illness could lead to a better outcome. However, have you thought about what really makes you sick? When you are cured of one particular illness, does it mean that you will not develop another illness? Not to mention that many diseases do not show early warning signs and, therefore, cannot be detected in an early stage. Then there are diseases that can't be successfully treated even when they are detected early on. In the worst case scenario, the checkup reveals a disease already in the terminal stage. When you find out that modern medicine cannot save you, where are you going to turn to then?

I am not trying to discourage anyone from getting regular health checkups or to sabotage your faith in them. What I really want to address here is that you can have regular self-examinations that are more effective, more meaningful, and do not require a single piece of advanced medical equipment. In this self-examination, you are to analyze your thoughts and your life by asking yourself how you feel. Are you living a happy life, or are you merely enduring life?

The more advanced modern medicine becomes, the more illnesses we find! We have become excessively dependent on pharmaceuticals, rather than rely on examining our thoughts. We have become a shadow of ourselves, an intimate stranger. We are blind to the high level of anxiety that we experience in our everyday lives. We are not aware of the large amount of depressing thoughts inside our minds. This is why many illnesses that used to be most prevalent in the very young and the elderly are now manifesting themselves in age groups that were considered to be prime health-wise.

The result of health checkups is to remind us that it is time for us to examine our inner world! Data generated from health checkup reports should be used as reference points: Are we living a happy life?

If the illness is cured on the physical level, but the mind still resides in a state of anxiety, sooner or later the illness will relapse. The real healing comes not from curing our physical bodies but from curing our spirits. Spiritual energy can alter physical realities. Pessimistic and negative thoughts are ultimately what causes cells to mutate! Only when we realize this, can we really heal illness.

If The World Were To End Tomorrow, What Would You Want To Do Today?

"If the world were to end tomorrow, what would you want to do today?" Does this question sound familiar to you? I am sure that we have all thought about it. If you were to die tomorrow, what would you want to do today?

Say goodbye properly to family and friends; eat whatever and however much I want; spend every penny in my bank account; confess my feelings to the one I love…. This hypothetical question sparks lively conversations, but, unintentionally, it leads to the actual realization of one's very own "Armageddon." This is when one hears the bad news from a doctor, "You have only three months left to live." All the bravado that was on display when it was only a hypothetical question is now forgotten. All that is left is hopelessness and sorrow….

When patients who face this "death sentence" turn to me for help, I always give them two options: "First option: Cry as much as you want for the entire three months and then pass away. Second option: Laugh as much as you can from now on, spend time with friends, go on journeys, enjoy fine cuisines, take painkillers whenever you feel pain, and enjoy life until the very end."

Choose to live a happy day over a sad one! "Easier said than done," many would say. But all that is needed is a change of mind!

Last year a story broke about a woman who was diagnosed with terminal cancer. It was said that she didn't have many days left to live. She decided instantly to sell her house and to withdraw all of her savings. She and her husband went traveling and just focused on enjoying themselves. Just when she had spent every last penny, her cancer cells were also found to have disappeared!

Her story is not one of a kind. Upon facing death, many people regret never really having lived. But what does that entail, "having really lived?" I have often said that all we need to do is to do our best and to live in the present. If we cannot even properly get through today, what's the point of worrying about the future?

Many of my patients facing terminal cancer took my suggestions to heart. They adjusted their lifestyle, striving to live everyday with joy. Guess what? Their cancer disappeared! However, another challenge arose. After finding out that they have basically cured themselves of cancer, some of them sunk into depression because they didn't know what to do next. Return to the battlefield of work? Face the troublesome relationships at home? Once again compete with everyone else?

This is it! This is the moment of truth! The foundation of the body-mind-spirit thinking is that we are required to live a life that is healthy, happy and worth-while. Our main job upon entering this world is to dedicate ourselves to lifelong learning and growing.

A real health checkup entails looking inside of yourself, examining your thoughts and your emotions, even those that have become deeply buried. When you become familiar with your thought processes and your natural way of reacting to the outside world, you can accurately assess the health status of your body. You will even be able to foresee future events.

"Children have the least amount of possessions but the largest amount of happiness; adults have the largest amount of possessions but the least amount of happiness!" This is because children don't worry too much about what the future may bring. They very much live in the present.

According to Seth's philosophy, it is a misconception that as we get older, we are more prone to sickness, cancer, and immune system deficiencies. It is true, however, that older people tend to be more pessimistic and anxious, that they don't feel as secure. It is these thoughts and not aging itself that weaken their bodies.

This does not mean that we should become paranoid and rule out any negative thoughts that we might have. The focus should not be to block out or repress negative thoughts. Instead, we should focus on obtaining a positive, cheerful and flexible outlook on life.

What makes human beings great is the ability to create our own lives! We can choose how much to be impacted by the external environment. We can also choose to change our thinking. We can switch positive and negative thoughts as easily as a flip of a coin. It is all in our hands!

Some live a privileged life, yet they feel nothing but pain. Some decide to end their lives just because of some comment someone made. Yet others live in poverty, but they still welcome everyday with a smile on their faces.

We are the ones who decide how to live our lives — sad and sorrowful or happy and joyful? We are the creators of our own reality. Each and everyone of us has the power to determine our own life.

 **with Dr. Hsu**

Question: We all have a dark side. How can we replace our negative thoughts with healthy thinking?

Response: First of all, keep learning. If you never make changes in your lifestyle, your thoughts will always be limited. You can only grow through learning,

**reading books and attending lectures. In this contin-
uous learning process, you will eventually come to
make sense of your thoughts.**

What exactly is healthy thinking? There is a saying that goes like this: "Black cat, white cat, any cat
that catches mice is a good cat!" Using this simple
comparison, any thought that leads to a beneficent
mood, frame of mind and physical condition is an example of healthy thinking!

Healthy thinking means trusting in the wisdom
of life. It helps us to open up our hearts. Healthy
thinking does not include hatred, conflicts, or self-
blame. Any thought that leads to pain is not a healthy
thought.

This does not mean that we should be afraid of
our own negative thoughts. A bad mood sometimes
works like a thunderstorm. Our true status of well-being becomes clearer after discharging the negative energy. By facing our thoughts, negative or positive, we
apply Seth's teachings in day-to-day living. This is how
"we create our own reality."

Thoughts not only alter cells, they also shape
your destiny. The more you are aware of your thoughts,
the clearer you can envision your future. Your inner
thoughts, emotions and imaginations (the causes)
grow into your physical world (the effects); that is the

holistic principle of cause and effect. We are our own creators! We are all divine creatures who came into this world to learn and to experience firsthand. We are apprentices on subjects of love, wisdom, inner senses, and creativity.

In the process of creating reality, we first create an imaginary world inside our minds using our thoughts, beliefs, emotions, and our individual perspectives on the outside world. Then we project it out into the physical world through our motivation and actions.

It all simply comes down to this: Pursue your dreams! Especially in this time and age, we need to learn to make our passions and vitality the leading force of our lives.

➤ Reminder from Dr. Hsu

Learning to trust is the most important lesson in life. Fear and distrust of the outside world lead to chronic sinusitis and allergic rhinitis. These diseases can be seen as our attempts to keep out the outside world. Deeply rooted fear and distrust penetrate deeper into the body and lead to pneumonia and lung cancer.

Now let's do this exercise. Concentrate on your lower abdominal area. Slowly inhale and exhale. Think of everything as a manifestation of kindness, including the universe, nature and all that's around you. Think of air as a warm supply of vitality. Then silently tell yourself, "I trust life. I trust love. I shall open myself fully with complete trust. Fully trusting, I will fill my lungs with love. I believe that my lungs will be totally healed by this unconditional trust and love! I am grateful for all of this." Keep repeating this exercise until you feel joy and peace throughout your body, mind, and soul.

Chapter 8
Kidney Diseases: Lay Down the Shield. Choose Trust Over Fear.

Urination is a natural physical need that we do many times in a day. We mostly notice the feeling of holding back the urine, urges to release it, or the relief after releasing it. In addition to the physical functions, how much do we know about the role that our kidneys play holistically in affecting our body, mind and spirit?

The Physical Functions of the Kidneys
The kidneys are a pair of organs located at the back of the abdomen. They are responsible for filtering the waste, mainly nitrogen, out of the blood. These wastes then become urine and are expelled out of the body after passing through the ureters, the bladder, and the urethra. During this process, massive amounts of blood run through the kidneys; therefore, they also play an important role in regulating blood volume, blood pressure, and some parts of the body's metabolism.

Creatinine and BUN (Blood Urea Nitrogen) are two common lab parameters used to evaluate our kidneys' functions. Our kidneys are not serving us well when they fail to filter out the nitrogenous wastes and to keep the nutritious proteins that our bodies need.

Kidney diseases, depending on which part of the kidney functions is failing to work, may have different symptoms such as proteinuria, edema, hypertension, as well as anemia. When the kidneys pass blood into the urine, in this process, hemoglobin is filtered out. Therefore, blood in the urine is a sign of disease. It is often found in the case of kidney inflammation, kidney tumor, or kidney stones. However, it can also be related to urethra problems or prostate gland inflammation and testicle issues.

The Story Behind Kidney Stones

People are told that their diet can be the cause of kidney stones, for example, eating spinach and tofu together or taking too many calcium and vitamin C tablets. However, these are just rumors, not facts!

While working as a resident doctor, I saw many kidney stone patients who suffered from severe pain. Among these patients I had noticed that most of them had one thing in common: They all seemed to be the key provider for their households.

My mother also had severe kidney stone problems, and one of her kidneys had to be removed. At the time she was diagnosed, she had just been married for a few years and was having a hard time trying to fit into her new role as a wife and learning to manage her family. Combining many years of my clinical experiences with the knowledge of the holistic principles, I realized that kidney stones are the symptoms of "helplessness." This could be helpless in regard to financial situations or to poor marital relationships. These people want to take a break from life, but they do not want to bear responsibilities. Practical concerns force them to be tough, yet deep inside they feel conflicted and stressed. Gradually, these chronic pressures grow into the "hardening stones."

Imagine how stressful it could be to walk around with an invisible rock in your back and not be able to remove it. The stress then forms the stones in your kidneys. Symbolically by expelling the kidney stones, we desire to release the invisible pressure. Pressures, fear and anxiety are inevitable in our daily lives. As a result we have to clean out accumulated pressures regularly by way of expressing our feelings. Pressures sometimes can push us forward, but too much of it is not a good thing.

Traditionally, men are expected to be the breadwinners for their families and should never show their vulnerability. They are face-saving winners who can only "grit their teeth" to cover their fragility and shortcomings. That is why kidney stones are more common among men.

Are men all "masculine?" The truth is that many times men also wish to be more "feminine," to need a shoulder to cry on, and to moan about how difficult and distressful it is for them to be so responsible.

Therefore, ladies, when your husbands are feeling down, do not scold them by saying, "What kind of man are you? Wipe your tears and be strong!" On the contrary, give them your support by listening quietly. If they can release their emotions, they can rebound from their bad mood and get back to their responsibilities. In most cases you don't even need to worry about whether or not you should go back to work and help in sharing the financial responsibility. Your husbands are seeking an opportunity to express their feelings. Once they are heard and understood, they will get back to work with joy. Psychological issues are meant to be understood rather than to be solved. A gentle pat on the shoulder with warm words to show them gratitude will serve as a comfort to them.

Kidney problems teach us to express our pain and feelings, as simply receiving lithotripsy treatment does not go to the bottom of the issue. Pressures do not disappear when you are hiding them inside. Worst of all, it proliferates. A kidney stone is the crystallization of chronic mental pressure. You should cultivate the good habit of cleaning out accumulated pressures regularly and also learn to locate the origins of those pressures. If you cannot eliminate the source of the pressure, at least, you need to clean it up regularly.

My advice is that you should have at least one or two close friends who are willing to listen to what you have to say. They don't necessarily have to offer you suggestions or solve your problems. They just need to be there for you while you talk so that you can release all of your pent-up feelings.

Body Intelligence to Cope with Our Environment

Ancient wisdom tells us that the body is formed by four elements of nature: earth, fire, water and wind. For tens of thousands of years, human beings have been coexisting and interacting with other beings in this world. These experiences have been passed down through our cells' memories for generations. This means that every human body is a sophisticated heritage fully equipped with the most advanced body intelligence to cope with our surrounding environment. Our bodies are capable of taking in any substance from mother earth that contains natural energy.

That is why holistic medicine believes that our bodies are born with a natural resistance against all germs and viruses. Our bodies have a complete immune system which enables us to digest any organic forms of physical or biological atoms and molecules from our living environment, including air, food, water, or even allergens.

Our bodies take care of all substances entering

our systems. So relax and trust your own body with everything, including your drinking water, small amounts of toxic residues from vegetables, and the air we breathe in. It appears that the medicines, viruses, and bacterias are responsible for damaging our health. However, long before that, the destruction to our health had already been made by our own negative energies. The real health killers are our negative thoughts and emotions that cannot be processed by our bodies, not the environmental factors. We are the ones responsible for the consciousness that affects our health, not viruses or bacterias. Otherwise, there should be no illness at all since we have already invented antibiotics.

When our bodies are doing their jobs in maintaining our health, are we doing our parts, too? Do we pay attention to whether or not we are producing negative thoughts and emotions every day? If we do, are we capable of releasing them?

If we fail to do so, our health will be on the line! Despite the fact that our body can handle the most vicious virus in the whole world, it cannot deal with the continual negative energies produced by our conscious mind.

One of my patients is probably qualified to be called a nutrition expert, because she has spent over ten years developing a healthy diet. Also, she has been eating nothing but organic veggies and fruits. Still, she was diagnosed with colon cancer.

She spent tons of energy and money on health foods but no time on her marriage. Her life was miserable because of her terrible relationship with her husband. She felt both sorry and annoyed for not knowing how to get along with him.

From her story we learn that no health diets in the world can fix your psychological issues. On the other hand, it probably enhances your chance of getting cancer. Strict diet control means that you don't have enough trust in your own body.

Many nutrition experts teach people how to select healthy food. However, our bodies naturally possess this ability. The only thing that we do need is to have faith in our own bodies, in the same way that we trust our own kids. The more you trust your kid, the better behaved he will be. If you want to be healthy, trust your body!

The world exists because we depend on each other. Without viruses and bacterias on this planet, human beings wouldn't be able to survive, either. This interdependent nature has never been recognized by Western medicine, which continues to believe that external factors are the source of our illnesses. It never realized the harmonious coexistence between our bodies' systems and the world.

As our conscious mind continues to dominate,

we gradually lose our bodies' natural powers. We need to learn how to readjust each organ and return our bodies back to a healthy state by way of altering our emotions and our thoughts. We all have the creative power within to achieve that!

Do Not Feed Your Kidneys with Fear

There is a Chinese idiom that says "Trembling with fear on the hearing of the wind." It describes how a person is so extremely terrified that he causes his gall-bladder to rupture. Even though it is an exaggerated metaphor for fear, I did encounter a patient whose fear literally blew up his kidney!

Mr. "Terrified Kidney" came to me because his creatinine level was 2.7 and his doctor had diagnosed him with kidney failure. He totally freaked out on hearing the news.

After further investigation into his medical history, I found out he had been searching for a medical cure since he was six years old. When he was six years old, he developed kidney problems after taking a Western medicine. He had lived in the countryside where advanced medical care was lacking. His condition did not improve for a long time. Only after taking an herbal cure offered by an old medicine man did his kidney problems disappear.

Because of this childhood experience that followed him around like a "shadow," he was always extremely careful regarding anything healthwise. He had every available health checkup done. Yet, by the age of forty-six, tests showed that he again had kidney problems. He felt as if his whole life were failing, just as his kidney had done.

In holistic health principles, kidney diseases are oftentimes related to fear and insecurity. You "feed" and grow your illness, just as if you were feeding the piglets and the chickens. My patient had lived for over forty years under the shadow of fear that his kidney would eventually fail. After all these years of feeding his kidney with "fear," how can his kidney not "fail" in order to "meet his expectation?"

This is also the main reason that the elderly have diminished kidney functions. Many elderly people often lack a sense of security. They live with the fear of loneliness, the fear of being discarded and cast aside. This mental attitude plays a more important role than aging. When you soak your skin in water long enough, it becomes pale and wrinkled. So imagine what will happen when you soak your kidney in a pool of fear?

"Let go of your fear if you want to improve your kidney problem." That's what I told Mr. "Terrified Kidney." Living in fear has no merit. It is detrimental to the quality of life and does not prevent the problem from getting worse. A kidney that is fed fear by its owner has no other way to go but to turn ill. Life goes on, with or without fear, so why not pick the happier choice?

Despite the fact that the human body is undoubtedly capable of dealing with the natural environment, it can be easily sabotaged by ongoing negative thoughts. Every once in a while, we need to reexamine our attitudes towards life and create a wholesome view of the body, spirit and mind. Frequently ask yourself these questions:

First, am I in a fearful and anxious state of mind? Second, do I have a strong enough faith in my own body?

After these two questions, relax. Calmly and slowly allow yourself to hear what life is telling you.

"You live in a safe universe!" This is the message that the Seth material brings to the world. We need to feel as if we are surrounded by a safe world. Also, keep in mind that your body is naturally healthy. That's the way it ought to be.

The Purposes of Natural Aggressions

More and more research articles and books tell us the same thing, namely that anger is a healthy and beneficial way of expressing emotions. Anger makes us take on the problem at hand and, therefore, creates the opportunity to change for the better.

Every emotion, including love and anger, is a form of natural aggression. The word "aggression" here is not to be used as in "attacking others" or in any other negative meaning, but rather a push toward "creativity." For example, when we feel passionate about someone, we express our love by freely extending smiles, hugs, letters or gifts towards them. This behavior is an act of natural aggression.

To Express and To Communicate Are the Purposes of Natural Aggressions

To show your anger is to let the other person know your feelings, not to attack him. Letting someone know that you are not comfortable with the way you are treated for the purpose of changing his treatment of you, that is "communication."

For example, if you were on a long bus ride and someone were to put his stinky feet on the back of your seat, I am sure you would find it very offensive. "The feeling of being offended" is an urge that reminds you to take action. You may politely ask that person to lower his feet. If he refuses, then you can ask the bus driver for help.

Following "natural aggression" does not mean to be angry with everyone. It is merely being brave enough to express your genuine feeling. For instance, take your annoying neighbor. He always parks his car in front of your house and blocks your exit. Not only did he not change his ways when you expressed your feelings of displeasure over his actions, he also gave you "attitude." Maybe you are an extremely tolerant person who really doesn't let him bother you. More often though, you are filled with anger. Rage is churning within you, yet you do not dare express that feeling. This is when the natural aggression comes into play. It is to help you claim your right. Let him know that parking his car is no problem. However, when he is blocking your exit, he is to move his car as quickly as possible.

We don't encourage bullying people, but neither do we wish to be bullied. When natural aggression arises, it is either expressed outwardly — or inwardly, which results in hurting yourself. Showing people that you are angry doesn't mean that you are a short-tempered person who can't get along with others. Instead, you are letting people know how you feel. Only then will people know how to treat you with respect.

Stand for your rights. Let others know your feelings, because this is the way to true harmony! Let people know where your boundaries are. Setting boundaries are, for example, "Don't put your feet on the back of my seat," or "Don't open my closet and take my clothes without my permission." Only when boundaries are clear, will peace settle in. Don't be the kind of person everyone steps on and disrespects at will. The more you make your feelings known, the more you will be spared hurtful experiences.

"Conflict" For the Sake of "Harmony"

Everyone probably knows someone they can't be around for five minutes without feeling extremely irritated. A person who had not gotten angry in five years probably has no lively energy at all! My former assistant was one of those people. I had known her for five years, yet I had never seen her angry. She was a dialysis patient. Some people have trained themselves and achieved a serene state in which they are not affected much by emotional turmoil. Most of these people, however, call themselves good-natured, but they are in reality only repressing the anger that is boiling inside of them. In the end this only leads to harming the body.

We all have our own unique ways of coping with "anger." Some people express their discontent freely, verbally or nonverbally by putting on a sour face. Some people turn to a third party to pour out all their frustrations. The worst way of coping is by burying all emotions. This is a major cause for kidney disease.

By carefully observing patients with kidney diseases, one finds that they often react in certain ways when encountering interpersonal issues:

First, in order to keep a harmonious relationship with people, they repress their anger.

Second, they use any means possible to hide their emotions from other people. However, inside there lives a bad-tempered, forceful self.

Third, they are often headstrong and competitive, yet underneath this exterior of bravado, they are afraid of conflicts and of being scolded.

Oftentimes, we are afraid to show our anger, because we lack a sense of security. For example, most kids throw their temper tantrums in front of their moms, not their dads, because they know for sure that their moms will still love them even if they are angry with them. Children often feel very secure in their relationship with their moms.

Children from alternative family units, as in the case of a stepfather, a stepmother or foster parents, are more prone to be insecure about their worthiness to be loved. The relationship between the new parent and the child is easily broken, because it is more difficult for them to see each other as family and to build trust between them.

Many kidney patients are bad-tempered. When growing up, they did not develop a strong enough sense of their worthiness to be loved. They did not feel secure enough to allow themselves to experiment with expressing their anger towards their loved ones. They are afraid. They think it's not safe to let their anger be known. Imagine you are furious with someone, yet you are too afraid to let him know: Where is that explosive pent-up energy going to go?

As I always say, "Negative feelings don't hurt anyone, except when they are repressed." Sometimes, conflict is necessary, but this only works when the relationship between the parties is built on love and trust. For example, if I am upset with you, why do I feel confident enough to open up to you and tell you how I am feeling? It is because our relationship has a solid basis of love and trust. When we have that, we feel free to share our most intimate thoughts.

There are two kinds of conflicts: One is meant to hurt each other; the other is to create greater harmony. The first kind is meant to hurt and attack the other party. It is not the kind of conflict that I recommend. The second one is for the sake of harmony. If I never tell you my true feelings, how are you going to know how to interact with me? Many animals mark their territory, not out of selfishness but for the sake of harmony. When boundaries are clear, everyone will know and respect their place. This is the great wisdom of nature.

Some people shy away from all conflicts with others, but they suffer inside! They carry pain inside them without the means to express it. For example, a man might be dragged out to go shopping. Even though he clearly doesn't want to go, he still follows his wife out the door without voicing his opinion!

A gentleman who works in a government agency came to my clinic for help. He was to undergo dialysis treatments. He reported going through life feeling a lot of stress. After further investigation through our sessions, it became clear that his stress originated from interpersonal relationships. He was upset about his colleague's work ethics, but he was too afraid to say anything. In fact he was so good at hiding his anger that no one had any idea what was going on inside of him.

In Seth's philosophy, there is nothing wrong with being angry, or even furious. They are merely emotions. The purpose of these emotions is to express your feelings to the person with whom you are angry. In this way, you can achieve a greater harmony within your relationship, instead of merely maintaining a superficial kind of harmony. Many people, however, achieve only this superficial kind of harmony because of their fear of conflicts. Then they suffer the consequences in silence.

At times in life, conflicts are necessary. When they are constructive in nature, they are a way of communication that allows us to express our feelings and opinions. Without them we cannot create greater harmony.

Let Feelings Flow

Feelings are never wrong or right. You feel what you feel. Does free expression of your feelings equal hurting other people's feelings?

I have a patient with a mental disorder who was deeply troubled by his "status." On his ID card his father is registered as "unknown," and his aunt is registered as his mother. It was decided for him by his elders that he would carry the maternal family name and that he would be officially adopted by his aunt. Growing up, he suffered from not knowing his father's identity. He keeps wondering about his lineage. Was he really a child whom no one wanted? It has haunted him all through childhood to adulthood. I suggested that he have the data on his ID card officially changed.

With a pained look, he told me that he was afraid that, by taking this action, he might hurt his aunt and the elders of his family.

I said to him: "When they made the decision for you, did they respect your opinion? Did they even think about the hurt that this decision might cause to a child's psyche? Not to mention that all you are asking is to put your biological parents' names on your own ID."

Often we fear that expressing our emotions will cause hurt to others, but we forget to take care of our own feelings. We do not have to worry about hurting other people's feelings if we do not intentionally and purposely set out to damage or insult them. Besides, whether or not one's feelings are hurt is a personal choice. If we always put everyone else's feelings first, how are we going to lead our lives?

Seth once told us that we all live in a big universe of love, in which no one will ever be abandoned or banished.

During one of my speeches, I mentioned that when I attended college I had wished my father were dead! My father was shocked to hear this when he saw the video of my speech. But afterwards he understood that behind my statement lay my deep love for him.

From a young age, I have been an obedient son, and I have always done my best to meet my father's expectations. Even after I attended medical school, I continued to struggle with the idea of becoming a doctor. My mindset of the time created a logic of its own: If Dad were to die, I would no longer have to struggle with this decision; if I don't have to meet his expectations anymore, I will be free to walk my own path in life.

Because I love him so much, I couldn't bear to let him down. His expectations triggered a battle of conflicts in my life. On the other hand, because I realized the depth of my love for him, I was willing to stay in medical school and continue to work hard. So, did my wishing my father to die come from love or hate?

Some kids may yell at their parents in anger: "I wish you would get hit by a car and die!" Expressing anger is neither wrong or right, but what this child really wants to convey is: "Dad! Mom! We are a family. I love you so much, and I know that you love each other very much, too. Why do you have to fight so much? Don't you care how sad I am to hear all this?"

When children express their true feelings, we need to learn to accept and to empathize instead of being overtaken by sadness or shock. Feel the love behind the words. Children more than anything wish for their parents to be happy together! If we have faith in love, we should be brave in expressing our true feelings. In the end love is the ultimate motivating factor. Only when we realize this will we be able to live joyfully and freely.

The holistic philosophy teaches us that, although we shouldn't use our thoughts to hurt other people, we also shouldn't sacrifice ourselves in taking responsibility for how everyone else feels.

The correct practice of the holistic principles is to take good care of both your body and your soul. You can only show love to others when you fill yourself up with love! If you feel sorry and angry about yourself every day, yet you are still worrying about how other people may feel, it is not "loving others" at all.

Don't be afraid to show your true feelings just

because you want to save face or because you are worrying about other people's opinions. You can only be responsible for yourself! Take responsibility for what happens to your life! Don't overthink it as long as you don't intend to harm or attack. When the powers of your body, mind and spirit are aligned, you will be your own master, holistically!

Lessons Learned From Our Kidneys

Our body, mind, and spirit work in sync. Through the manifestation of kidney disease, we learn the true meaning of "feelings."

Feelings are a form of natural aggression, for the purpose of expressing ourselves and communicating with others. Sometimes, they may appear to cause a conflict, yet they are not meant to cause harm to others. On the contrary, they are meant to achieve greater harmony. Therefore, we should communicate our feelings to the people around us, instead of bottling them up inside and letting them fester because of fear and insecurity.

We live in a safe universe, in a state of grace and love, in which not a single person is left behind! Miracles are everywhere, every day, according to Seth!

Kidney diseases are irreversible from the viewpoint of modern medicine. However, from Seth's holistic perspective, human bodies are miraculous! The human potential for recovery has no limits! Some organs have remarkable regenerating powers. For example, after having their appendices removed, some people manage to grow a new appendix. Miracles are made only through the change of your beliefs. The self-healing process is only activated when you shift your inner perspective. So from now on, stop worrying about when your kidneys will fail, because fear will only speed up the failing process!

Allow people to know how you feel. Believe that to express yourself is to communicate, not to attack or hurt other people. Do not be afraid to express your feelings. Let them flow spontaneously.

As for your health, pay less attention to the outside and focus more on the inside, that is, your spiritual self. This is a journey of continuous learning. In order to be happy and healthy, we need to keep on learning and growing. That's the vision of the future to which we are looking.

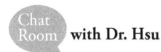 **with Dr. Hsu**

Question: My child has had three surgical procedures because of congenital urethral stricture. Now he is facing degenerative kidney dysfunction. How can I help him deal with these problems mentally?

Response: If all these medical treatments have already been done, then the next step is to work on the spiritual part. From now on provide your child with a different outlook: "You are perfectly fine, my child. You are healthy physically, mentally and spiritually! We have done the work. From now on you are free from any kidney disease. Live your life as if you had never been sick."

The most important thing is to give the child faith and courage. Allow him to express himself in front of everyone. Let the illness be the turning point which allows him to be even happier than before he became sick. The power of utilizing the holistic principles regarding health is quite powerful. As I have said many times before, the occurrence of a congenital disease in a family is not random. There is a reason behind it. I'm not talking about negative karma like a punishment as many would believe. The child bearing the congenital disease has chosen deliberately to reincarnate into this particular family; the reason for his arrival may very well be to bring out the courage of the mother!

Maybe before she had her son, she was a timid person, someone who always shrinks back into the background. Now faced with her child's illness, she has started researching on her own, finding the right doctors and resources, determined to fight his illness. For her child's sake, she has risen up and shown bravery and strength!

A child is a gift to the family. The interactions between the parents often change after a child is born. People often discover their strengths after becoming parents. Naturally, there will be many differences in opinions, but by dealing with them, they hone their skills in communication and mutual understanding.

When it comes to illnesses, it involves more than the person in question. It affects the whole family and the family dynamics. If the parents instill courage towards life in their child and provide the guidance for him to find his own way, the energy and dynamics within the family will change for the better, and the kidney will start to function better and better!

➤ Reminder from Dr. Hsu

Here are some questions for you. Are you constantly holding back your complaints and your anger in your relationships with friends and family members just to keep the peace with everyone? Is there a timid, frightened self living inside of you who is fearful of being scolded or being blamed? Have you been trying hard not to express your true feelings just because you are afraid of conflicts?

Well, stop running away and stop repressing your feelings. Restore your faith in life and have the courage to believe in yourself. Be your real self and feel free to express yourself. Believe with all of your heart that your body will speed up its recovery once the energy passages inside of you are all clear.

Chapter 9
Suicide: Taking on Feelings of Powerlessness in Life

When talking with people who contemplate suicide, I will empathize with them. I will tell them that I understand their desire to be freed from the ongoing pain inside, a pain that feels excruciating every single second of every day, but that I disagree with them that suicide is the way to go about it. I will tell them: "It is true that we don't have a method to alleviate the pain right this minute, but come on, you have hung on for so long. Please hang on a little bit longer.

"You are wonderful; you are brave! If I were you, maybe I would have given up a long time ago. It is really a big deal that you have made it this far….." These are words from the bottom of my heart, and I always make sure to say them out loud to those patients who are contemplating suicide.

Throughout the course of life, almost everyone has had thoughts of escaping challenges through death at some point or another, especially in those moments when we feel frustrated and defeated by life. It starts as a whisper, "What's the point?" Then it grows in strength. Although from the perspective of holistic health and Seth's philosophy, we absolutely do not encourage suicide, we also do not condemn suicide as some of the religious or community groups do.

Seth considers people who died by suicide as people who were desperately in need of help. Not only shouldn't they receive extra punishment after death, but they should be given extra guidance! This is what sets Seth's philosophy apart from the traditional view. Traditionally, those who committed suicide are considered sinful and thought to be creating bad karma. It is believed that after death they will get severe punishment, and in the next cycle of reincarnation, they will degrade to the animal realm.

Personally, I think that the only right way to deal with death is to consider the dying process in a natural and dignified manner. This is why I don't approve of euthanasia. What we look for is dignity and quality of life. We must respect the truth that where there is life, there is death. In the face of death, we should not always resuscitate against all costs. The brink of dying is a very special moment, where fighting desperately to preserve the physical shell might be disrespectful to life!

One Person's Death Is a Warning to All Others

Recently, several cases of primary school children committing suicide have been reported. These tragedies do not only happen in Taiwan but all over the world. If I were the school principal, teacher or a parent, this is the question I would ask myself, "What have we done?

What makes children who should be happy and care-free at this young age instead feel so miserable that they need to end their own life?"

Does the school lack a sense of warmth? Is everyone in the school so indifferent to one another? Do we only care about grades and overlook the children's need for support, care and love?

Every single case of suicide is a warning to us! The ones who needed to learn and grow were not only those who committed suicide! It's us! Why couldn't we, the living and breathing ones, establish a family, a society worthwhile for them to want to stay alive?

The rise of the suicide rate indicates the dysfunction of society as a whole. This is like a company that is always hiring new employees but with a high turnover rate where all of the new hires do not stay long. There must be something wrong with the company itself!

Not only do people committing suicide have to face their own issues, but the entire human race also needs to take a hard look in the mirror! We may not know the child who killed himself. He may be someone else's child, but he is really a child of all of us. If the boy next door can commit suicide, how can we be sure that our own child won't do the same? We can't put all the blame on the ones who chose to end their own lives. When the tragedy happens, we all feel the hurt inside, just as if it were our own child who had ended his life!

The same goes for adults who commit suicide. In the case of an older adult, we should feel as if the deceased were our parent, our grandparent or someone else in our family. Never should we look at it as some singular anonymous case. Only when we accept the deceased person into our heart, will we have learned the important lesson.

Life can be a hard journey, but however hard the journey is, we push on! We set foot on this earth to experience every obstacle of life and to learn to overcome it. Let's join hands and connect to one another, when one of us commits suicide; then it is a moment of reflection for us all.

More Compassion, Less Blame

A person with suicidal thoughts needs empathy and support, not just to be stopped. Having experienced countless failures in life, he already considers himself a loser who can't succeed in anything or get approval from his family. When his last resort to escape agony through death is frowned upon by his closest relatives, it is no wonder his suicidal thoughts grow in strength!

A person with suicidal thoughts usually has one last line of defense: Someone who hears what he is trying to say!

What he needs the most is someone who listens, someone who listens quietly when he talks about his regrets, pains, and grievances, someone who looks at him with empathy and understanding and without any judgment. "There is still one person in this world who understands me! There is still one person who is willing to listen to me and who doesn't judge me." This feeling is often what changes the minds of those on the brink of committing suicide and which encourages them to hang on to life a little bit longer! It is because there is still one person who cares.

Simply saying, "Don't kill yourself!" never works!

When talking with people who contemplate suicide, I will empathize with them. I will tell them that I understand their desire to be freed from the ongoing pain inside, a pain that feels excruciating every single second of every day, but that I disagree with them that suicide is the way to go about it. I will tell them: "It is true that we don't have a method to alleviate the pain right this minute but come on, you have hung on for so long, please hold on a little bit longer."

People with suicidal thoughts need empathy and understanding, not disagreement and judgment. The nature of life is joy, and life is meant to help us experience and grow through these experiences.

The Souls that Need More Care

Throughout human history, many people have died by suicide. Broadly speaking, even "soldiers who died in action" can be seen as committing suicide.

Almost without exception, people who succeed in suicide regret their impulsive action. On a spiritual level, the greatest harm to their soul is eternal regret. Their souls will be stuck in a closed off vicious cycle of regret and self-blame. This is the real danger of suicide!

The afterlife is not painful at all; the pain lies in realizing the huge mistake that cannot be reversed! The moment they realize that they have succeeded in killing themselves and are unable to return to the realm of the living, they risk a total breakdown.

Seth speaks about guidance counselors in the afterlife, who look after those people who have committed suicide. These counselors have developed a unique technique. They use hypnosis to bring their "patients" into a dreamlike state. In this state, they relive their suicide attempt but this time with a different outcome: They fail in the attempt. For example, while trying to hang oneself, the rope suddenly gives way. Or just when one is about to jump off the train platform, the suicidal person gets knocked off-balance by someone trying to catch the train.

When someone attempts suicide and fails, usually he won't make a second attempt anytime soon because he will experience relief at still being alive. Only when the overwhelming pain returns, will he then make another suicide attempt. The technique used by the afterlife counselors brings the suicide victims into a state in which they believe their suicide attempts have failed, allowing them to go through the emotions of relief and regret: "Why did I do that?! Why was I so determined to die? I am so lucky that I didn't succeed!"

Physically, the suicide victim has passed away, but his soul and consciousness have entered a different realm. He starts to question — what was so terrible that could only be solved by death? Is a romance gone bad or a cheating spouse worth taking his own life? Slowly, he will realize that he still has many people who love him. Why should he die for people who don't appreciate him? Has he been too self-absorbed in his own pain that he has overlooked the feelings of those who do care about him? After a while, he will come to his senses, and he will be thankful that his suicide attempt failed.

Many people who enter the afterlife can't at first tell the difference between being alive and being awake in a dream. The afterlife counselors will wait until their consciousness has stabilized in the afterlife before telling them the truth. "We know you are now ready to hear this; we have to tell you the truth. The truth is that your suicide attempt was successful! You are no longer among the living."

After the first shock wears off, they will benefit from having already worked through the regrets, the inner conflicts, and the self-blame. Now their souls can finally rest in peace!

Why make all these efforts to guide those suicide victims into slowly realizing their true condition, namely that they're dead? It is because no suffering is worse than having a restless soul! All souls long for peace! Even after death, after passing over to a different realm, you can obtain peace of mind. This is the love and compassion that shines through in Seth's philosophy.

All of Us Have Had Thoughts of Giving up on Life

When facing the ups and downs of life, I have always had this feeling: You get more of what you cherish most! On the other hand, you lose the things to which you have not paid enough attention. Only when you have treasured something will it truly belong to you.

We often only appreciate something after we have lost it! Often, only after we have lost someone we love, do we ask ourselves whether we have adequately expressed our love. Do we cherish our children for who they are instead of their accomplishments? There are so many layers of emotions and feelings which we can explore and learn to express.

I often plead with people not to see suicide as a mortal sin. On the spiritual level, suicide is like the wife who is fed up living with her husband and his family, and who, in a fit of rage, runs back to her parents. In the heat of the moment, she does this because in her eyes her parents represent unconditional love. On the spiritual level, in a way, committing suicide is similar to throwing a tantrum!

Emmanuel, a New Age master once said, "First of all, I would like to salute all the souls who have decided to come into this world."

Every soul who chooses to be born into this world must have tremendous courage! It is an honor to be a human being. This is what sets Seth's philosophy apart from other traditional religious beliefs. Seth believes that to be born into this world is an honorable choice, not the result of punishment nor should we be considered "fallen." Only the bravest souls dare to venture here!

Our world is filled with challenges – comparison, competition, and discrimination. But these hardships do not exist in the spiritual world!

Buddhism's teachings say that human life (or the human body) is precious! It is precious not because it takes many reincarnational cycles to enter this human realm. It is precious because among the trillions of choices in the universe, we chose to be human. Therefore, we should be proud of ourselves for having the courage to be human! We should change our perspective on life and often remind ourselves that we are great and remarkable!

In the mortal world, death means the end. In the spiritual world, however, it is never too late! The universe is compassionate, and it will always provide second chances until we have learned the true meaning of life. These second chances are not punishments at all; they are love. These chances provide every wounded soul an opportunity to heal! For either the living or the departed, one day, we shall be united with our loved ones once again. However far the distances, the love between us will never be lost!

Retaking the Course of Life
When we were in school, we might choose to drop out when we cannot overcome difficulties. Similarly, some souls decide to drop out of the school of life and return to the spirit world.

The universe is compassionate and understanding about the dropping out. Nevertheless, the missing credits cannot be skipped. As a result, those dropouts will be born again to retake their course and face the obstacle from which they once ran away! Human beings will never be reborn as animals, because the soul needs a human body to learn to cherish and confront life.

What kind of new life will those who drop out of life by means of suicide have? First, they will be given the courage not to give up. There are a lot of people who, while struggling in a survival mode, show an incredibly strong will, whether they are physically disabled, severely injured in accidents, or terribly sick. Some of these souls had experienced suicide. The stunning willpower is probably the outcome of continuous building up of courage after several suicides.

For those who drop out due to suicides and then return, there is a firm inner voice that tells them never to give up! No matter what, they will make it this time! Deep inside his soul, he knows that he had chosen to die by suicide, running away from the battle of life too many times. So this time, he decides to press on!

Second, they will gain an understanding of losing loved ones. Those who previously committed suicide may reincarnate and encounter a different perspective of suicide: the suicide of a loved one. This is not a punishment, but it is meant to trigger the soul's deepest understanding about life by losing someone he loves. "I love you so much! How dare you leave me?" Ironically, he had done the exact same thing to someone else! When putting himself in the opposite position, it makes it more personal. He has the opportunity to reflect seriously and to determine never to give up quickly in future life experiences.

From a broader perspective, we can see that all those who committed suicide not only died for themselves but all of us. They represent all of us who are still suffering and choose to die because of that. Their deaths remind us of our own sorrows and force us to face our own life issues, whether it is family affairs, romance challenges or career obstacles, anything that makes our lives too bitter to swallow. All those painful emotions can be brought back to the surface by one man's death!

Hence, I will say, "New life has risen from the ashes of death!" The suicide of one man awakens us to look into our sorrows and to face life again. By this opportunity, we release the inner suffering and gain the inspiration to live again. Thus, the meaning that suicides bring is divine! While we do not agree with suicide as a tool to solve problems, we are grateful for those who use their own lives as the wake-up calls for the world.

Suicide and Karma

"Suicide" and "karma" are usually considered as the cause and effect. Within this context, I must redefine "karma." Our lives cannot be determined by the karma of our past lives.

For example, let's say there is an ugly man. He is told by a "great master" that because he was such a handsome man in his past life, he was born ugly in this life as a punishment for being good-looking before. That way he can learn to appreciate inner beauty.

Here I must share an important concept: The current-life you is not the past-life you. You are not punished because of anything in your past life. The point of power always lies in the present. Even though both lives belong to the same entity, you are still two individuals, free of the attachment of karma. In addition, what you learn and how you grow in this life can help the past-life you.

You decide how your appearance is, not because you are forced. It is an active choice made by your own free will. You should learn to seek your inner value and not be attached to your outer appearance. Furthermore, you can find the one who loves who you are, a lover who can see your true nature through the unpleasant appearance. This is the subject your soul longs to learn.

The experience and wisdom gained by the "ugly you" in this life can also contribute to your other lives. So, I don't think being ugly is a punishment. Instead, for the "other you" who was once obsessed with his own beauty, being ugly can expand his spiritual experiences.

There is no original sin or karma, and we are only responsible for our present life! Every life is a new beginning for the soul; we all start from scratch without the burden of the previous mistakes coming after us. These rules apply to those who committed suicide as well. It is alright to drop out of school. However, sooner or later, one will need to retake the course until he learns the meaning of life.

Children Reveal it All

I once had a depressed child as my patient, and I discovered that his mother was also depressed. She often wanted to commit suicide! Interestingly, the mother told me, "Dr. Hsu, I hide my depression so well that my child doesn't even know I want to commit suicide." What this mother didn't know is that her child was sleepless every night in order to keep an eye on her. Some other parents came for my help because their children want to kill themselves and could find no meaning for life. What lies beneath the child's suicidal thoughts is that the parents could find no meaning in their marriage. They would have divorced if not for the children. Subconsciously, the children will perceive the message and think of their existence as the only reason keeping their parents together. So the child will start to become depressed, maybe even suicidally depressed; he doesn't want to be the excuse of his parents' not freeing themselves from their marriage.

Many people may think that children are too

young to understand, yet children know all the secrets kept by the parents! So whenever you see a depressed child, you must try to explore what his depression is trying to convey.

To truly help a depressed child, one must be honest with himself and the child. Because adults cannot deal with what is going on, the children suffer. The key to a successful education is honesty, not white lies. Depression is just the starting point to tell the story buried deep inside. There is no other way, but to explore the cause and essence of the depression. This is the only way the child can be helped.

Understanding the Nature of Depression

I like to joke about what depression is: You feel relaxed and carefree when you close your eyes in bed at night, leaving all your worries behind. On the contrary, you feel like hell when you open your eyes again the next morning, thinking about all the things you have to or all the problems you have to face.

Unlike bipolar disorder and anxiety, the symptoms of clinical depression are a low mood, negative thinking, a lack of sleep or inability to be interested in anything, loss of appetite and always wishing to stay at home.

About 80 to 90 percent of people with suicidal thoughts are diagnosed with depression. Thus, many experts are starting to educate people about how to recognize the signs of depression. By emphasizing the advantage of early diagnosis and regular medication, they wish to lower the suicide rate and cure as many depressed people as possible.

However, according to Seth, all emotions are good! Depression itself is not a disease at all. All emotions, if freely expressed, can promote spiritual growth. That includes anger and depression as well!

The Upside of Depression

Unlike many other problems, in my point of view, depression can be beneficial in two ways: First, depression keeps you away from suicide. Pathologically speaking, those who are in deep depression won't try to kill themselves because their energy level is simply too low to do so. Also, when a person is in deep depression, he is indecisive. It might take hours to choose which clothes to wear before going out.

A cook, who is also my patient, can usually make a dish in 30 seconds. But when the depression strikes, he barely knows what to put into his pot. As a result, one cannot commit suicide at the bottom of his depression. What worries the psychiatrist the most is when a patient slowly starts to rebound from the bottom of his mood swing or slightly gliding down the curve from a temporary summit of recovery. These are the periods when a patient is most likely to decide to end his life.

Most suicide cases occur when the patient leaves the mental hospital. They are no longer a mentally ill patient, and they have to confront their problems now. They find it so unbearable that it leaves them no choice but to put an end to life! Yet, they have not yet found the solution to their inner issues.

Second, depression improves your holistic health. Often we press on in life and ignore how we feel. Depression requires us to slow down and to take a step back. We ask ourselves, "Why am I depressed?" It is because we encounter challenges and obstacles. Depression makes our soul hibernate temporarily, just as nature adjusts according to the rhythms of the four seasons.

Think of your life as a speeding train. Depression is like the gate at the railroad crossing, reminding you to stop, look and listen. Depression is constructive for your body, mind, and spirit!

A person suffering from depression might seem to lack energy, lying on the bed all day. However, this is time for spiritual integration. This is a chance to explore yourself, to find adjustments to your life, to reflect on your life, and to change your stubborn thinking.

Sometimes a detour is the best way of releasing yourself from a dead end. Depression is like a detour in your life. It is time to take a break, to confront your fragility and frustration. Depression is constructive at the holistic level!

The worse thing to say to someone with depression is: "Stop being depressed. Cheer up and get on with your life!"

Usually, this is what I will say instead to my patient, "It is okay to be depressed! Don't worry about it. Take as much time off as you need."

Your body needs rest when you are sick; your soul needs rest when you are depressed. Your soul needs a recharge. Depression is your intelligent auto-adjustment where "afflictions are none other than enlightenment."

Depression is the result, not the cause. It is not just about the depressive episodes; it involves all the previous inner causes building up into the result!

Seth once told us: "Affirm yourself during your depression."

Depression is a time for self-reflection! You should think about how hard you have been pushing yourself and others. You should realize that you are too proud to admit failure. Depression makes you listen to your inner voice and to let go of the past without self-denial!

For example, a father had always wished that his son become a doctor and his daughter become a lawyer. He demanded that they study harder and harder to meet his high expectations. One day, his children finally couldn't take it anymore and said to their father: "Father, even though you have given life to us, we are not your property. We have the right to decide our own futures. Stop controlling our lives!"

Being accused, the father went into a depression! Not only would his wishes never come true, but he was also depressed because his children didn't appreciate everything that he had done for them.

Depression reminds the father to examine if he had done anything inappropriate? He started to reflect, "Is this the best for my children? If it is, why did they hate it so much? Did I really do it for them, or was it for my own good?"

All of these questions might never have been asked if it were not for his depression. We can be so stubborn about what we believe... until depression knocks on the door. Depression is here to promote our spiritual health. Don't push it away with antidepressants: We need to elevate depression with our spiritual wisdom!

With depression, we can ask ourselves, "What am I insisting on? Am I pushing myself into a dead end? Is someone forcing me? Or am I trapping myself by my own beliefs? Does my own attachment tie my hands?" Depression will take your soul to its deepest sorrows, then opens another window in order for you to change.

The wisdom you can learn from depression is that you are your own life saver! Depression is not a monster or a demon, nor an illness that you are eager to cast away. Depression can be your best friend, a messenger. Fluoxetine (Prozac) does not have the answer to your life, but your depression does. Listen attentively to what your depression has to say.

Depression Lets You Get Away With Anything

In my clinic, I have seen many depressed women. One of them is a very responsible person who spent all her days taking care of her in-laws and kids, while her husband cheated on her. First, she was full of rage; she couldn't accept that all her hard efforts were rewarded with her husband's betrayal! She was unhappy and became depressed.

I told her, "Your depression is good for balancing yourself. From now on, if your in-laws are good to you, then be good to them because it's reciprocal! You are not doing this for your husband. He will have to fulfill his own duty as a son!" I then want her to ask herself why she feels mistreated. Does she feel that she has to sacrifice herself for others? Then I tell her, starting now, to take the time to enjoy a tea time with her friends or to watch movies to relax.

Depression helped this woman not to work too hard and not to burden herself with unhealthy emotions that can lead only to regrets if she gets cancer someday. Depression made her reexamine her life, and it allowed her to build a more reciprocal relationship with her in-laws instead of taking responsibilities on all by herself.

That's why depression drains your energy and makes you unmotivated in every way, temporarily. It allows you to look back at your life and ask yourself if that is what you really want.

Take me, for example: If one day I were suddenly to become seriously depressed and start whining to my parents, "You are the ones to blame! I didn't want to become a doctor. I only did it because of you! You have ruined my dream of becoming a singer," then I might cry and wail as much as I want, regardless of my perceived self-image. Depression gives me full authorization to become totally unreasonable, and through that process, I can regain balance.

Fundamentally, depressions are different from suicides. Depression is a turning point in life, allowing for learning and growth; depression is a complete sense of helplessness! Many people are often mistaken about the difference.

It is a dangerous move to ask a depressed person to get well soon. He is depressed because he can't accept his current life. Depression is a gesture of getting away by asking people to be considerate. He is figuring out his life! Depression is just the explosion of his accumulated imbalances, which he can never dare to express!

Depression is an outlet for an inner sense of helplessness and negative energy. It is just like the pus due to infection; you have to squeeze the pus out to make it heal. Hence, medications that control emotions but fail to understand the essence of depression can only deepen the sense of helplessness and, therefore, raise the suicide rates. In studies regarding teenage suicide cases, the statistics indicate that some antidepressants promote suicides. When the medications block the last outlet of depression and the doorway of the soul's energy is cut off, people are more prone to commit suicide.

Trust in life, in yourself, and even in your depression. Follow it through, and it will lead you to your limiting core beliefs. If you let your days drift away or you deceive yourself that everything is fine, know that these are signs of avoidance and pretending to be strong.

Depression guides you to see your stubbornness and attachments. For example, my own stubbornness may be that I have to be a doctor to prove that I am a good son. Does that mean that, if I am a singer, then I am a bad son?

For many of my homosexual patients, their parents only find out about their children's sexual preference when their children are hit by depression. In the end, their parents choose to accept their child's sexual preference, because they would rather have a gay child than a dead one!

Again, depression is like a baby throwing a tantrum: "This is not funny! I don't want to play anymore! It's none of my business. I no longer want to feel this pain. I want to be who I am and be the master of my life!" Life cannot rebound without hitting bottom. To rebound from the valley of depression, you have to embrace yourself truly.

From the perspective of Seth's philosophy, depression allows the soul to see the silver lining of a rejuvenated future. If suicide is the end of the journey of life, depression restarts your journey. Only the hibernating winter of the soul can bring the prosperous spring of life.

The Ultimate Purpose of Life

As Seth told us, all life has an ultimate purpose! If you find your life meaningful with a special mission, no matter how difficult life becomes, you won't give up easily. On the other hand, if you find life meaningless, it doesn't make sense to stay alive. Why should you bother to endure any longer? You are not motivated to fight back when life beats you down!

It is not a coincidence that our soul lands on this world. Sometimes, the purpose of our life is coated with a layer of bitter obstacles. The purpose inside of you is yelling at you and says, "Life is good." Let's listen to the voice inside and find the ultimate purpose of our lives.

 with Dr. Hsu

Question: Can suicide reports on the news stimulate more suicides?

Response: When there are massive suicide reports on the news, there will be more people committing suicides during that period. People think this is a side effect of overreporting. Suicide news encourages those who have already thought about committing suicide to make the final move and those who are not considering suicide start to think about it. However, I must clarify that no suicide reports can cause a suicide trend! No one will take his own life if he is under the sole influence of other people's deaths. He will not commit suicide unless he has already had the idea to do so!

Not a single suicide can sprout into action without the seed of thoughts already having been planted.

Question: How do we lower our sensitivity to the environment such as weather changes or noise distractions?

Response: When you are emotionally unbalanced, something small can trigger an explosive reaction. For example, if you become extremely impatient with your husband when he is continually nagging you, you might lose your temper and begin yelling at him. This is a sign to let you know that your emotions are out of balance.

Everyone should develop the habit of finding outlets for their emotions. There is a practice in the Seth philosophy that can help you to maintain your holistic balance: Integrate yourself into your surroundings.

For instance, once when I was on a plane, we encountered turbulence. I got very tense and had no idea what would happen next. So I started Seth's practice. First, I let go of my ego. I imagined that I was the wind and that the wind was me; I was the rain, and the rain was me. I began to feel more relaxed once I let go of my ego and my fear and I started to integrate myself into nature. I was no longer nervous but felt a sense of security.

The trick of this practice is to free yourself from your personal identification and to bond with the force of nature. This process builds a connection between your inner self and the universe; rain and storms are manifestations of our own force.

When you feel emotionally dragged down by the weather, the best thing to do is to integrate your emotions with the weather. Imagine that your emotions are here to carry away your worries, just like the rain and the storms are washing away all the dust and dirt.

➤ Reminder from Dr. Hsu to Those with Suicidal Thoughts

I understand your feelings when having these suicidal thoughts and feel deeply compassionate about how painful it is for you. But is it totally hopeless? Do you have to commit suicide today… or within this week?

Look, I can't command you not to do it, but can't we wait awhile? Since you already want to kill yourself, does it matter if we postpone it until after Christmas? Or maybe until your birthday next year? Let's wait and see if things will get better. You have nothing to lose, so why not give it a try?

Chapter 10
Hypertension: Choose Flexibility Over Perfectionism

People often ask me, "Is hypertension a hereditary condition?" My answer is, "It might be, and it might not be!" We all know that heredity is related to genes. From a holistic perspective of body, mind, and spirit, however, we can mend faulty genes through a change in our thinking. The fact that our parents or grandparents suffer from hypertension, diabetes, cancer and various other diseases does not mean that we are high-risk candidates to inheriting these diseases!

Hypertension has already become a worldwide epidemic disease. Both at home and abroad, many globally leading countries hold particular interest in this so-called silent killer. Various diseases that are linked to hypertension, such as heart ventricular hypertrophy, coronary heart disease, stroke, retinopathy, and kidney failure, instill fear in the general public.

Before going into depth on the subject of hypertension, let's first talk about the basics. Our heart works as a pump that generates pressure to move the blood to the entire body. When our blood pressure is measured, the nurse will name two figures, the so-called systolic and diastolic blood pressures. When the heart contracts, it pushes out the blood into the arteries which causes the arteries to expand. The pressure that is built up within these expanded arteries is the systolic blood pressure. Diastolic blood pressure, on the other hand, is measured when the heart is relaxed and, thus, causes the pressure in the arteries to drop to its lowest point.

A systolic blood pressure between 110 and 140 mm Hg and a diastolic blood pressure between 70 and 90 mm Hg are considered normal. However, this norm may not fit people of Asian origin, especially the women. Asian women are slimly built and are often not as focused on physical fitness as Western people. Therefore, I often promote the following concept: The standard for blood pressure is not absolute; one should always take one's self as the most important reference point!

Hypothetically speaking, if my systolic blood pressure is usually around 90 to 100 but one day it goes up to 135, I should start to pay attention, to monitor it to see if my blood pressure is too high. For anyone else, 135 might be a normal score. Therefore, everyone should have a general idea of what his normal blood pressure is. However, if your blood pressure is usually 135 but one day you measure 150, don't be too worried immediately. This one higher-than-usual measurement may have been the result of not having slept well the night before or, perhaps, because you just had a fight with someone.

Many factors can contribute to the change in blood pressure, including our total blood volume. When our bodies produce urine, they filter out blood through the kidneys, and so the total amount of blood inside our bodies will decrease. Think of it as a water tower that is low on water; the water pressure will go down. Therefore, diuretic medicines are used for the purpose of controlling hypertension. Other factors that influence blood pressure include contraction of the small arteries and regulation of the kidney functions.

It is often advised to lower one's salt intake. This is because salt increases the osmolality (the concentration of a solution) in the blood, causing the total blood volume to rise and, therefore, the blood pressure to increase. But keep the following in mind: When you increase the salt intake of a healthy person, he will not develop hypertension. Only when a genetically predisposed person takes in too much salt, will he be at risk of developing hypertension. So getting used to being on a low-salt diet at a young age does not mean that one will never develop hypertension later on in life.

One can wonder if unlimited business opportunities don't, in fact, motivate many of the medical concepts today. Just keep in mind that many factors influence blood pressure. There is a correlation between overeating salt and having high blood pressure; this does not mean that too much salt causes hypertension! Even within the body of one person, blood pressure will change. With aging, blood pressure will change.

Modern medicine does not really understand hypertension. If only we knew the root cause of this disease, then we should be able to find the cure! So far modern medicine can only "control" hypertension, but they are not doing a very good job of that. If hypertension is well controlled, older patients will not suffer from complications. If not well controlled, the patient can only blame himself for not having taken the medicines accurately, on time, every time. Needless to say, these drugs will need to be taken for the rest of his life!

Antihypertensive drugs are only effective in lowering blood pressure; they do not provide the cure. Compare this to the example of an adrenal gland tumor: The tumor will continuously produce adrenaline which causes blood pressure to rise continually. Once the tumor is removed, the blood pressure will lower. Modern medicine, however, still does not have an explanation for the adrenal gland tumor in the first place.

Shifting Perspectives to Alter the Genetics

In the early days, if any member of a family was a cancer patient, the whole family tried to hide it as a deep dark secret. The main concern was that it might affect their children's chances of a good marriage. This was because their future in-laws might have worried about their offspring contracting cancer through the odds of heredity. Nowadays, cancer is as common as the flu, so people can only live with it and carry on with the fear of this "heredity."

I am often asked if hypertension is a genetic disease. My answer is both yes and no. As we all know, genetic diseases are related to genes, yet, in Seth's philosophy, genes can be rewired by shifting our beliefs. The hypertensions, diabetes or cancers of our parents or grandparents don't automatically impose on us a higher risk. It does not mean that we have a predisposition in our genes!

If one of your family members is having hypertension and you have heard that it can be genetic, then you have probably implanted the thought hypnotically!

For example, if a man knew his mother had hypertension when he was twenty, and people told him that it can be genetic, then unconsciously he was deeply hypnotized, and the signs of his own hypertension started to show in his thirties.

A suggested thought implanted into your subconscious starts to influence your physical body. So it's essential for us to build on the concept that our body will not be taken control of by those unwell genes unless we choose to accept it as truth! Recently, I gave suggestions to my mother when she was worried about her high blood pressure readings by telling her, "This is only temporary. You might have exhausted yourself too much lately, but it will be better when you rest more!"

Once the word "temporary" sneaks into her subconscious, it starts working immediately! Hypertension is only temporary; it is a phenomenon that will get back to normal soon enough.

In Seth's philosophy, you create your own reality. Your personality defines your illness and your destiny!

When you are taking antihypertension medicines, it means that your blood pressure will go higher if you don't control it with medications! This is because you <u>believe</u> that your blood pressure will continue to go up or stay high. This is no doubt a suggestion and deep hypnosis.

Our personality is affected by genes. However, our personality can also modify our genes. The learning of holistic health concepts is like an engineering project of genetic maintenance, although not the kind of genetic project done in a lab. It is a project to implant new concepts and beliefs into our consciousness and subconsciousness. When we make up our mind to change the perspective of our thoughts, the genetic heredity has been altered.

Knowing that every word can enter into the listener's subconsciousness, I never say anything with negative suggestions in it. This is because I know how critical negative suggestions are to negative physical conditions.

When we are trying to give a positive suggestion, don't forget to "sugarcoat" it. For example, I told my mother, "An elegant lady such as you will never have the problem of hypertension!" She was flattered to hear this, even though hypertension has nothing to do with being elegant. To bundle an old thought that is convincing to someone with a new thought that you wish him to take in is the technique of hypnosis. This is how to make suggestions work!

From now on, walk out of the shadow of "genetic heredity." Because when you are accepting this new concept, your genes are also evolving simultaneously!

Don't Rush Yourself into Hypertension

"Do you know Fulong, our neighbor next door? She had a stroke, and she is only fifty, you know!

She can no longer use her arms and legs….She always rushes herself into everything." When I have some free time to spend with my mother, she never forgets to update me on all the news about our neighbors, friends and relatives, "Oh, and your auntie! She also had a stroke many years ago! Slightly bulky, I thought she was a laid-back person who always goes along easily with everyone, but not after I saw the way she talked to your uncle and her kids. She was talking and rushing on about everything. She looks like an entirely different person to me!"

I can't help but smile when I hear my mother mention "the rushing personality." She can see the "rushing" factor instead of other characteristics; this means that she is learning from me subconsciously! As I always say, "All the chronic diseases are related to one's personality, especially for people with hypertension, who like to rush things!

There are two types of people who like to rush: The first kind not only has to rush everything, but he also demands that everyone else go at his pace. These are the obvious kind. The second kind is more subtle. You can't tell from his appearance that he is rushing into something. He quietly pushes only himself without bothering other people.

For these rushing people, if you delegate work to them, they will finish it as soon as possible…. If for some reason that is not possible, then they will constantly worry about it. If he can't achieve the results he wants, he will not dare to leave the office, or he might just take the work home to continue.

These people may be the favorites of all bosses.

Realistically, there are millions of tasks in one person's lifetime. If we try to keep everything in mind and rush to finish everything, then we are building up our blood pressure! When you are taking a taxi and you tell the driver: "Please hurry! I need to catch a flight!" Then you will see the driver gets tense and focuses on driving at full speed. His blood pressure is probably also running at "full speed" now.

Normally when you are in a hurry, your blood pressure goes up, but then it goes back to normal when you are not. For people with hypertension, they are always in a rush, and their "ups" never come down if the work isn't finished. Then here comes the next task, adding more to his mind, and more "ups" are added. Gradually, the blood pressure keeps piling up. It builds up from 70 to 100!

Therefore, your blood pressure is not built to the height of a skyscraper in just one day! It takes years of rushing emotions to form an invisible state of mind! This is the root cause of hypertension.

Are you worried about not being able to hurry through anything anymore? Don't be. If you are too laid-back and lack the desire to rush something, you probably won't get to finish anything in your life.

It is normal to want to speed something up. When an exam is coming, of course, you are waking up in the middle of the night spontaneously to study.

If you have an order to deliver, of course, you are pushing every procedure in order to send out the cargo. Then, what are the differences that make it okay or not? The point is:

First, do you have to do everything now?

Second, if you can't do it now, does it bother you?

For instance, the mother asks her child to take a shower. If he hasn't done it in ten minutes, then the mother gets annoyed! It's reasonable to feel rushed or pressured while you are trying to multitask. On the other hand, will the child be suspended from school because he didn't shower on just one day? Why not try to loosen up a little and lower the standard? Why not allow him to take his shower before bed? If the mother wants him to take off his clothes so that she can do the laundry, then she might buy him more clothes or make him wear dirty outfits to school. If he doesn't like that, then he will go shower before he runs out of clean clothes.

You are only punishing yourself by hurrying your kids every other minute! Some parents don't seem to discipline their children. However, they know in their mind what's yet to be finished. This is the underlying (second) kind of rushing I mentioned before.

Sometimes we are rushing out of worry for things that may never happen! If your kid can't get out of bed in the morning, then allow him to be late for school a few times. After a while, he will take responsibility for getting ready for school on his own! The more autonomy we allow our children, the more disciplined they will become. If you are trying to be responsible for him, he will throw everything on you because he cannot do it in his own way.

So let's review the characteristics of hypertensive people: One, they have to do things now. Second, they are always worried about how things are going. Furthermore, they get angry when other people do not cooperate with their schedules.

Is it the end of the world when things are not done? No. All these highs and lows of their emotions are burning up their blood pressures.

A worried mother came to me for help because her son likes to use dirty language. I told her, "Your son will stop it only when he thinks it's not good."

Then she brought her son to me. I asked him to tell me some dirty words. The boy was astonished and asked, "Are you going to write it down on my medical records?" I nodded. He went silent for a while and then said, "It doesn't sound pretty…."

Afterward, he thinks about our dialogues every time he is about to speak the dirty words. Naturally, he tries to hold it back. If he had never realized the fact that they are not pretty words, he wouldn't have stopped saying them no matter how hard his parents scolded him. On the contrary, he would have done it more often to irritate his parents intentionally. He was doing it just for rebellion's sake. So be a wise parent: Quick words of blame can only do harm to your relationships.

A really smart parent is the one who stops being responsible for their kids when they grow up. If you have a teenaged rebel, the only thing you should do is to show him or her your love. They can choose whatever they want to do; however, they must be responsible for themselves. You will fail if you are trying to rush your kids. They have to "rush" themselves.

The Sun Always Rises

Several years ago during one of my public speeches, a young lady was sharing her experience of how she was diagnosed with hypertension when she was twenty-eight years old. She was describing her struggles, how she could barely breathe while walking up to the entrance of the cardiology department. She said this was because, in her viewpoint, cardiology is for older people. Then she got diagnosed with left ventricular hypertrophy caused by hypertension. By the time she was telling this story, she had already been taking anti-hypertensives for nine years.

In her family, she had an irresponsible father and a mentally ill mother. Her grandmother had been taking care of the whole family until she died. The young lady took over her grandmother's duties and became the "adult" for her younger siblings. She had no grownups to help her along the way; she had had to grow up facing all the nervousness, anxiety, and helplessness on her own. Despite her school friends being at her side to listen to her problems, they couldn't offer any real help.

Being an "overachiever," she became even more responsible after she started to work. She has "rushed" everything into completion so perfectly that her boss gives her all the tasks, even those that should have gone to others, and leaves her in charge. She doesn't like her current job, but she does not know how to change her career path. She feels as if the end of the world is coming!

For many hypertensive patients, they were all going through a tough time facing undesirable yet necessary things before they were diagnosed. In addition, there is no one else to help. If they don't have anyone else with whom to talk, they can only bury their anxiety inside.

I always recommend having someone who can listen to all your worries. Whether they can help solve your problems or not, to be able to talk it out already lightens the burden.

Or you can find a quiet, comfortable place to relax. Indulge yourself at a spa, watch a movie, or take a coffee break at the corner shop, etc. The point is to be good to yourself. All these activities help you relax your body and mind.

If you have ever had a cat, you will know that cats like to lay on the floor with their tummies up and enjoy the feeling of the gentle touches of others. If suddenly the cat spots a cockroach, it will jump up immediately to give chase.

We can learn a lot from the behaviors of animals. When you pet a cat, her throat will make a purring sound to show that she is very relaxed. The cat can instantly switch from relaxation to tension. It is totally fine with her. However, once a person is tense, it takes a long time to become relaxed again.

I like to promote the idea of giving massages between parents and kids or husbands and wives. It is a very good activity for our health; it works especially well for hypertension. When our skin is gently touched, our body will release endorphins which relax the brain, and that feeling will go through the whole body and mind. It works better than ten antihypertensive pills!

I have been leading so many people on the journey of holistic principles for learning and growth that sometimes I wonder what would happen if I were no longer here? Then I will mock myself after that! If that day really comes, the sun will still rise, and the flowers will still blossom. Those who are fond of these beautiful concepts will carry on and be even more successful. What am I nervous about?

Cuddling in my cozy bed, I imagine this with my eyes closed, happy and contented. Even if tomorrow is the end of the world, today, I am still here, and the flowers are still blooming under the warmth of the sun.

Why are we afraid of tomorrow? In our worries, tomorrow has come to be today and then became yesterday! Despite every sleepless night spent worrying, the sun will still shine on your face in the morning. But your blood pressure will have gone up because of your sleeplessness.

We may never be able to cut bitterness out of the joy right away. However, we must learn how to blend in the bitterness with our joy! Things are not usually as bad as you think they are, and taking a short break won't collapse the whole world. To heal your hypertension, you have to start from developing your character. Learn to slow down and ease up. Take life not too slowly but not too fast, either…and definitely not too worried!

The Point Is Not How Much You Regretted It; It's How You Deal with Regret

Many times we are looking for trouble. You can't do everything without having the regret of missing something! The point is not how much you missed; it's how you deal with it!

Some people are always wearing sorrow on their faces, frowning. They don't smile that much, and they are never content with life. Most of them live in pain and with regret, sacrifices, and bitterness during their lives.

Seth had many reincarnational experiences as human beings. One of them was as a female beggar who had twelve kids, all with different fathers. She and her children wandered around the streets begging for food. However, no matter how poor they were, every morning was a surprising triumph to them because none of them had died from starvation during the night. Over time, she looked at her children playing, and she was happy! She was so grateful to the world.

Seth, as a beggar, experienced a high density of satisfaction, even higher than that of his other life as a Pope. As a beggar even bread crusts tasted better than any of the fancy cakes he had eaten in other lives.

It is so easy to be content. Also, it is so easy to find a million excuses to stay unhappy. The unhappiness of modern man is not caused by deficiency but by greed. We cause our pains by dissatisfaction and always looking at the negative side. When we cannot improve our situation, we become cynical, and it costs us both our happiness and our health.

To be content doesn't mean that you don't want to make progress. On the contrary, because you are more than satisfied with what you already have, you automatically attract more to you! Because when we are thankful for everything we have, we show gratitude to our beautiful days. When we smile because we can sleep comfortably in our cozy bed, then this state of satisfaction will connect us to the state of grace from the universe. A man with a contented smile on his face will never have hypertension!

We tend to overlook the core issues and think only about the surface problems. For example, which one do you really care about: How your kid feels, or how good his grades are? How your spouse feels, or is he having an affair?

How many things do we put upside down in prioritizing in our daily lives? How many times do we have to argue about where to eat, how we squeeze our toothpaste tube, or should we put down the toilet seat or not?

We are all different people who are meant to have different opinions. If we have to care about every single detail for months, our bodies will become overwhelmed. Let's get back to the inner essence, to where the fundamentals are. If I buy a car to replace my legs and to enjoy driving, then let's not focus on worrying about the scratch on it that makes us sick.

On the journey of life, sometimes we forget what we came for. Rewind yourself to the root of that first thought, and you will realize that you can be happy. Now.

 with Dr. Hsu

Question: I had been drinking and smoking since I was in junior high school. Even though I have quit the habit for almost six years, recently I started to smoke again just to enjoy the mood. Is that bad for my health?

Response: People always ask me about the relation between exercise and health, and my typical answer is, "Your attitude towards exercise weighs more than the exercise itself."

I am not a smoker, but I do occasionally drink some red wine before bed to relax. Holistically speaking, if someone is drinking with a sorrowful mood, then he is turning the wine into tears that are toxic to the body.

On the other hand, if he is drinking with joy, singing and laughing, or even crying and talking about what's going on in his mind, then he will still wake up as healthily as he has always been. In a word, whether drinking is influential to health depends on the mood: Are you happy or sad?

Alcohol can be both good and bad for one's health. A small amount of alcohol helps us to release our emotions and become more relaxed and at ease, as long as it doesn't turn into an addictive substance. In some primitive tribal cultures, they consider alcohol to be sacred! Alcoholic drinks are only offered in traditional festivals as a symbol to express their gratitude to heaven and earth, and as part of the celebration ceremony, It represents an event in that everyone gets together, drinking, dancing and laughing. In that case, it is a beneficial activity for the health.

Sadly, modern people don't drink that way. They use it as an anesthetic to avoid their bitterness, and that is harmful. What's even more harmful is the unhappy heart. So the influence of alcohol varies. Some people can open themselves up to talk because of the alcohol; then this is also a way to heal themselves.

The same applies to smoking. How do you feel when you smoke? When someone gets nervous, he lights up a cigarette because it helps lower the anxiety and calms the nerves. Smoking can't be beneficial to him if it is used to put himself into a stupor of his own feelings.

Drinking and smoking are neutral activities if used with adequacy and a bright mood. However, when they become tools for escape, dependency or even self-abandon, they can be a greater danger to the health.

Again, your mindset speaks louder than your actions. If you set your mind right, everything will be right for you.

➤ Reminder from Dr. Hsu

Hypertension is highly related to subconsciously suppressed anger. So the first question on your self-checklist is, "What do you honestly feel?" For example, is the communication in your marriage depressing because it is like a debate you can never win? You simply don't have enough arguments to support your thesis, while your spouse is dominating the game because he or she has the superior position and has brought in more money to your family? You feel as if you have to make way and give up on your needs all the time, which builds up a sense of rage and helplessness inside. The truth is that you are furious about yourself; you blame yourself for not being successful enough and for acting like a loser.

If you fit in any of these descriptions above, you have to replace these feelings with recognition, acceptance, and transformation. Allow the negativities inside to be released out of you; otherwise, the negativity will continue to build up into a sense of helplessness, and eventually it will turn into the diagnosis of hypertension.

An Introduction to Seth

The Spiritual Teacher Who
Launched the "New Age"Movement

Who is Seth?

Seth is the internationally acclaimed spiritual teacher who spoke through the author Jane Roberts while she was in trance and whose empowering message literally launched the New Age movement. The books written by Seth have sold over seven million copies and have been translated into a dozen languages. Seth's clear presentation of the furthest reaches of human potential, the eternal validity of the soul, and the concept that we create our own reality according to our beliefs, has rippled out to affect the lives of people in every corner of the globe. Seth's work (first published in the late 1960's) has withstood the test of time and is still considered by many to be one of the most comprehensive, brilliant and undistorted maps of inner reality and human potential available today. If you want answers to life's most important questions, if you want to improve your life conditions, Seth's books will show you how, not by relying on him, but by accessing and using the tremendous source of power and wisdom that lies within each of us.

Reviews from Leaders in the Field of Human Potential and Consciousness Studies

The Seth books present an alternate map of reality with a new diagram of the psyche... useful to all explorers of consciousness.
   —Deepak Chopra, M.D., author of *Ageless Body, Timeless Mind* & other bestsellers

I would like to see the Seth books as required reading for anyone on their spiritual pathway. The amazing in-depth information in the Seth books is as relevant today as it was in the early '70's when Jane Roberts first channeled this material.
   — Louise Hay, author of *You can Heal Your Life*

I count Jane Roberts' brilliant book The Nature of Personal Reality as a spiritual classic and one of the influential books in my life. As I closed the last page, I looked up at a new world—boundless and filled with possibility.
   —Dan Millman, author of *The Way of the Peaceful Warrior*

Re: The Nature of Personal Reality: A Seth Book
Quite simply one of the best books I've ever read.
   — Richard Bach, author of *Jonathan Livingston Seagull*

Seth was one of my first metaphysical teachers. He remains a constant source of knowledge and inspiration in my life.
   — Marianne Williamson, author of *A Return to Love*

"The Nature of Personal Reality: A Seth Book" had an important influence on my life and work. Seth's teachings provided one of the initial inspirations for writing "Creative Visualization."

— **Shakti Gawain, author of** *Creative Visualization*

The Seth Books were of great benefit to me on my spiritual journey and helped me to see another way of looking at the world.

— **Gerald G. Jampolsky, M.D., author of** *Love is Letting Go of Fear*

As you read Seth's words, you will gain more than just new ideas. Seth's energy comes through every page, energy that expands your consciousness and changes your thoughts about the nature of reality.

— **Sanaya Roman, author of** *Living with Joy*

If you are interested in learning about the Seth material, we recommend starting with the three books below or visit our educational websites.

SETH BOOKS by Jane Roberts

The Seth Material
Seth Speaks
The Nature of Personal Reality

For further information and a complete list of Seth books, online courses, conferences, Seth Audio CDs and MP3s, visit our websites:

www.sethlearningcenter.org
Introduction to Seth, free audio clips of Seth and free CD or MP3

www.sethcenter.com
The Seth Bookstore, Seth books and audio CDs & MP3s the complete works of Jane Roberts

www.sethinstitute.org
Online Courses & Conferences

To request our free catalog or for further information contact us at:
Email: sumari@sethcenter.com
Phone: 516-869-9108

THE SETH AUDIO COLLECTION

THE SETH CLASS SESSIONS (1972-79) are available on CD or MP3 along with transcripts. These are audio CDs and MP3s of the actual Seth sessions recorded by Jane's student, Rick Stack, during Jane's classes in Elmira, New York, starting in 1972. Volume I, described below, is a collection of some of the best of Seth's comments gleaned from over 120 of the later Seth Class Sessions. Additional later Seth Class Sessions are available as The Individual Seth Class Session CDs or MP3s.

For information ask for our free catalogue or visit us online at www.sethcenter.com.

Volume I of The Seth Audio Collection consists of six (1-hour) cassettes, CDs or MP3s plus a 34-page booklet of Seth transcripts. Topics covered in Volume I include:
• Creating your own reality – How to free yourself from limiting beliefs and create the life you want, • Dreams and out-of-body experiences. • Reincarnation and simultaneous time. • Connecting with your inner self. • Spontaneity – Letting yourself go with the flow of your being. • Creating abundance in every area of your life. • Parallel (probable) universes and exploring other dimensions of reality. • Spiritual healing, how to handle emotions, overcoming depression and much more.

Order The Seth Audio Collection at www.sethcenter.com New Awareness Network, P.O. Box 192, Manhasset, NY 11030. Or Call (516) 869-9108 9:00-5:00 p.m. Monday-Friday ET

For the complete collection of Seth Books and Audios visit www.sethcenter.com

Books by Jane Roberts from Amber-Allen Publishing

Seth Speaks: The Eternal Validity of the Soul. This essential guide to conscious living clearly and powerfully articulates the furthest reaches of human potential, and the concept that each of us creates our own reality.

The Nature of Personal Reality: Specific, Practical Techniques for Solving Everyday Problems and Enriching the Life You Know. In this perennial bestseller, Seth challenges our assumptions about the nature of reality and stresses the individual's capacity for conscious action.

The Individual and the Nature of Mass Events. Seth explores the connection between personal beliefs and world events, how our realities merge and combine "to form mass reactions such as the overthrow of governments, the birth of a new religion, wars, epidemics, earthquakes, and new periods of art, architecture, and technology."

The Magical Approach: Seth Speaks About the Art of Creative Living. Seth reveals the true, magical nature of our deepest levels of being, and explains how to live our lives spontaneously, creatively, and according to our own natural rhythms.

The Oversoul Seven Trilogy (The Education of Oversoul Seven, The Further Education of Oversoul Seven, Oversoul Seven and the Museum of Time). Inspired by Jane's own experiences with the Seth Material, the adventures of Oversoul Seven are an intriguing fantasy, a mind-altering exploration of our inner being, and a vibrant celebration of life.

The Nature of the Psyche. Seth reveals a startling new concept of self, answering questions about the inner reality that exists apart from time, the origins and powers of dreams, human sexuality, and how we choose our physical death.

The Unknown" Reality, Volumes One and Two. Seth reveals the multidimensional nature of the human soul, the dazzling labyrinths of unseen probabilities involved in any decision, and how probable realities combine to create the waking life we know.

Dreams, "Evolution," and Value Fulfillment, Volumes One and Two. Seth discusses the material world as an ongoing self-creation—the product of a conscious, selfaware and thoroughly animate universe, where virtually every possibility not only exists, but is constantly encouraged to achieve its highest potential.

The Way Toward Health. Woven through the poignant story of Jane Roberts' final days are Seth's teachings about self-healing and the mind's effect upon physical health.

Available in bookstores everywhere.